I & II Timothy / Titus
FOR BEGINNERS

MIKE MAZZALONGO

THE “FOR BEGINNERS” SERIES

The "For Beginners" series of video classes and books provide a non-technical and easy to understand presentation of Bible books and topics that are rich in information and application for the beginner as well as the mature Bible student.

For more information visit: **BibleTalk.tv**

ISBN: 978-1-945778-85-8

BibleTalk Books
14998 E. Reno
Choctaw, Oklahoma 73020

TABLE OF CONTENTS

I TIMOTHY

TABLE OF CONTENTS

I TIMOTHY

The two letters that the Apostle Paul wrote to the young evangelist, Timothy, provided him with clear instructions for the divinely ordained way the church of the New Testament was to organize and function not only in the first century but throughout history to this day and beyond.

1. INTRODUCTION TO I TIMOTHY

I Timothy is the first in a group of epistles (I & II Timothy and Titus) written by Paul the Apostle and addressed to ministers, unlike his other letters that were directed toward churches (i.e. Ephesians, Corinthians) or to specific members (i.e. Philemon). Because they mainly deal with ministers and their work in the church, these writings have been referred to as the "pastoral" epistles by various scholars, the thought being that through these letters Paul was pastoring or shepherding these young preachers and guiding them in their work.

Today the pastoral epistles not only guide us in our Christian walk and direct us in the proper way to organize the church, they also provide the qualifications to look for when selecting spiritual leaders and define the basic work of the evangelist/preacher/minister in the local assembly.

I Timothy — Background

Before we look at the letters themselves, it would be helpful if we examined some background information to better understand the context in which Paul was speaking at the time.

Time period

When studying various epistles that describe events in the church of the first century we have to take into account the period of its development at the point of writing since it went through several important phases in a very short time. For example:

1. **Inception period** – This took place on the Jewish feast of Pentecost, shortly after Jesus had ascended into heaven. At that time 3000 people were baptized on hearing Peter's first sermon concerning the death, burial and resurrection of Jesus Christ. This event established the church in Jerusalem (Acts 2:36-47).
2. **Expansion period** – The church continued to grow in Jerusalem, but after a time expanded from its base in that city to neighboring towns and bordering countries. The great breakthrough came, however, when the Apostle Paul and his associates brought the gospel to many parts of the Roman Empire and churches were formed among the Gentiles.
3. **Consolidation period** – At this point in its development the focus was on internal growth with the appointing of local leaders and an emphasis on church organization. For example, it was during this period that churches became self-supporting, not needing external help to financially maintain its ministers and work. Also, local ministers like Timothy and Titus were taking charge and thus lessening the burden for teaching and preaching that had been done by the Apostles and early missionaries.

I mention these three general periods because in his letters Paul deals with issues and problems encountered by churches in the consolidation period when assemblies were in the process of training and establishing leadership positions within the church. I and II Timothy and Titus are specifically addressed to two preachers who were working with churches that were already well established. I believe that studying these epistles will give us a view of the early church and its development, and will also guide us when selecting those who will serve as ministers, elders and deacons in the Lord's church of our day.

Background

There is not a lot of information concerning Paul's first imprisonment in Rome, but it seems that after spending several years in Roman detention he finally went before the Emperor to plead his case and was successful (62 AD). While he was in prison, Paul's intention after his release was to go to Jerusalem for a time and then return to Rome to strengthen the church there and, finally, press on to Spain in order to open up new frontiers for the gospel. Once released, however, his plans changed. He did not go to Spain during his brief time of freedom, instead he chose to spend time in Crete (Titus 1:5), travel to Ephesus (I Timothy 1:3), return to Corinth (II Timothy 4), Miletus (II Timothy 4), and to Troas (II Timothy 4:13). It seems that he used his freedom to revisit and encourage established churches instead of moving on to plant new ones.

The letters to Timothy and Titus suggest that Paul was free and actively working with these men and other preachers to strengthen established churches as mentioned previously. In II Timothy the tone and situation will change. Paul will once again be in prison and this time will not have great hope of being released on account of the rising tide of Roman persecution.

During this brief period of freedom, however, Paul wrote this first letter to Timothy, a young evangelist, working with the church at Ephesus.

Who is Timothy?

We first encounter Timothy in (Acts 16:1) when Paul was on his second missionary journey. Timothy was a native of Lystra located in what was then Asia Minor (modern day Turkey). His mother, Eunice, was a Jewish Christian who along with her mother, Lois, raised Timothy to know the Scriptures which eventually led him to be converted. Timothy's father was Greek and a non-believer. This young man was converted by

Paul (I Timothy 1:2) and he joined the Apostle's missionary journey in 51 AD.

Timothy's call to ministry was indicated by God (I Timothy 1:18), and he was commended to service by Paul and the elders (I Timothy 4:14). Along with Luke, he was one of Paul's closest traveling companions and served in many capacities but eventually was sent to Ephesus to minister to this fast-growing church.

We also know that he spent time in prison with Paul (Hebrews 13:23) and that he was timid by nature not dealing well with confrontation. He was also a man who suffered from stomach problems (I Timothy 5:23). Paul loved him like a son, was lonely without him and always worried about his condition. Tradition (not the Bible) says that Timothy died as a martyr under the reign of Nerva or Domitian. He was also believed to be a co-worker of John in this Apostle's later years.

This letter is personally addressed to Timothy while he was working with the church at Ephesus.

Ephesus

Ephesus was the place where Paul had enjoyed some of his greatest success during his 54 to 57 AD missionary effort. He had written to this church while in a Roman prison between 61-62 AD and then, after his release, visited them for a time and left Timothy there to minister. Paul had planned to return but was detained in Macedonia (northern Greece), so he wrote this letter to Timothy giving instructions about how the church should function and how an evangelist should minister to the church.

At the time of Paul's ministry in the second half of the first century, Asia Minor with Ephesus as its main city became the numerical and geographical center of Christianity. In 70 AD Jerusalem was destroyed by the Roman army. This made Ephesus, with its many Christians and churches, an influential place for believers to gather. Paul had established a church there, missionary efforts to plant other churches in the region had been launched from there (i.e. Colossian church - Epaphras), Timothy was sent there to minister, and after Paul's death John the Apostle settled and pursued his ministry from this place.

Large public church buildings did not appear until the 3rd century, so early Christians met mostly in homes and in private meeting places. Each of these house-churches had its own leaders and each guided their own group. Paul is writing to Timothy about the conduct of these churches and the type of men needed to lead them during the difficult times they were experiencing because of persecution from the Roman government and division caused by false teachers promoting heretical teachings concerning the gospel.

Authorship

The material contained in all three epistles suggests that Paul wrote these letters. Some people doubt his authorship claiming that the pastoral letters are the work of a later author, however Paul's name is used to introduce several doctrinal ideas. Some doubt Paul's authorship claiming that certain events mentioned in the letters do not fit with similar accounts described in the book of Acts. The response to this is that these letters were produced after the events written about by Luke in the book of Acts took place, and nothing in these letters contradict statements made by Paul in other New Testament epistles. In addition to this, there were no accusations of false authorship mentioned by church historians concerning these letters since they were universally accepted as legitimate early in church history.

Outline

I Timothy is a mixture of personal encouragement and teaching along with general instruction for the church at large. For this reason I Timothy is not easily structured into neat sections since Paul moves from one topic to another. Here is the outline I will use in our study:

1. Greetings – 1:1-2
2. Paul and Timothy – 1:3-20
3. The church and prayer – 2:1-15
4. The church and leadership – 3:1-16
5. The church and apostasy – 4:1-16
6. The church and different people – 5:1-6:2
7. Final appeal – 6:3-21

Why Study I & II Timothy and Titus?

Here are some of the benefits that we receive in reading and studying the pastoral epistles today.

A. They are one of the few source documents that teach about church administration and organization.

B. They stress the importance of knowing and teaching sound doctrine.

C. These letters demand holy living of both leaders and church members.

D. They provide historical information about Paul and the church that we might not have otherwise.

E. In these letters God speaks to the church today as He did then.

Heresy at Ephesus and Crete (I Timothy 1:1-3)

Paul writes to Timothy to help him deal with various issues that have come up in that congregation. Since Paul cannot be there in person, he provides Timothy with instructions that will guide the young evangelist in teaching and properly organizing the church that he serves at Ephesus.

> [1] Paul, an apostle of Christ Jesus according to the commandment of God our Savior, and of Christ Jesus, who is our hope, [2] To Timothy, my true child in the faith: Grace, mercy and peace from God the Father and Christ Jesus our Lord. [3] As I urged you upon my departure for Macedonia, remain on at Ephesus so that you may instruct certain men not to teach strange doctrines,
> - I Timothy 1:1-3

One of the motivating factors for this letter may have been an earlier meeting that Paul had with elders from Ephesus and the surrounding region while he was traveling to Jerusalem (Acts 20:17-32). During this meeting Paul encouraged these men to be diligent in carrying out their ministry and warned them to be wary of false teachers and their influence in the church (Acts 20:29-30).

It seems that despite Paul's warning, false teachers still managed to infiltrate the church and cause problems. The first letter to Timothy, therefore, deals with false teaching that had invaded the church at Ephesus which this young minister now had to contend with. Timothy needed to stand up to these heretics and provide correct teaching to counter or neutralize their errors.

The false teaching itself was complicated and not the type of thing that we are familiar with today. Understanding the nature of this heresy, however, will help us more fully appreciate Paul's teaching in this letter.

The Heresy

The false teaching was referred to as Gnosticism. This term comes from the Greek word "gnosis" which means knowledge or "to know." Gnosticism was produced by the mixing of a variety of knowledge sources. They mixed ideas from Greek philosophy (Plato), concepts from mystic and pagan religions, added teachings from Judaism as well as Christianity, all of which taken together produced a different gospel message. They promoted their teachings as a type of "super" gospel, but in reality their message was only partly true. One of the concrete doctrines produced by this Gnostic approach was something called "Dualism."

Dualism taught the following:

A. There were only two elements in the world: God/mind, matter/flesh.

B. Both of these were eternal in nature.

C. God/mind was good and matter/flesh was totally evil.

D. Human beings were a combination of the two.

  - They had flesh, therefore they were totally evil because the flesh corrupted the mind.

E. They taught that in order to obtain salvation, the spirit in man had to escape the flesh in man.

  - When this was done the spirit/mind of man could return to God where it belonged and be at peace.

F. They also taught that there were two different ways that this escape from the flesh could be accomplished:

  - **Strict asceticism** - (I Timothy 4) which included:

i. Food laws
ii. Forbidding marriage
iii. The spirit had to dominate the flesh - The error here, of course, was the false notion that one could be saved by works of the Law (the Jewish Law) or of the flesh and not by grace through faith as Paul had originally taught them (Ephesians 2:8).

- **Antinomianism** (complete indulgence of the flesh)

  i. No law or restrictions
  ii. Complete sensual freedom

In essence they taught that since the spirit and flesh were separate, one didn't affect the other so a person could do what they wanted in the flesh without affecting the spirit, which would ultimately be free once the flesh died.

The error here was that according to the gospel, a soul could not sin without consequences from God who judged and punished all sin (Romans 6:15).

It wasn't bad enough that this Gnostic doctrine of dualism was circulating in the church, what made matters worse was that people were arguing and debating these things!

In addition to the spread of these doctrines, there were two destructive features being created in the character of those who were embracing these false notions.

Speculative Intellectualism

The first of these was an incessant discussion and argument about matters that the Bible didn't even address rather than the study and the discussion of what it actually taught.

- What will I look like in heaven?

- What did Jesus look like?
- When is Jesus coming back?

Intense examination of biblical gossip, traditions, myths, genealogies and ideas which some people thought were important but not biblical, much like the interest in the "Shroud of Turin" or the "Da Vinci Code" movies and books today.

These things make for good entertainment perhaps but have zero value in the Christian's understanding of salvation or effort at righteous living, serving others, or glorifying and pleasing God. These type of things then and now only generated endless speculation and arguments without edifying anyone. They were majoring in minors and this led to the second deadly attitude that was affecting the church at Ephesus:

Pride

Pride is the root of most false teaching. Some are too egotistical to submit to God's word or too lazy to study it. Others are too proud to admit error and too stubborn to change.

In Ephesus some false teachers had the vain conviction that only they had access to the special gnosis, this secret knowledge, and thus only they could show others the way to receive it. This, of course, was not only wrong, it was dangerous.

> 16 All Scripture is inspired by God and profitable for teaching, for reproof, for correction, for training in righteousness; 17 so that the man of God may be adequate, equipped for every good work.
> - II Timothy 3:16-17

Dangerous because this attitude created pride and competition among teachers, and a resistance to hear the teaching from the Apostles or others, like Timothy, who had been trained and sent by the Apostles. Paul, knowing about these issues, writes to a young minister who is trying to cope with these disruptions in the church.

Timothy is young, he's unsure of himself, he has a nervous stomach and he's facing men who are proud and argumentative about their new and superior knowledge, their new "gnosis."

Paul writes to challenge, instruct and provide Timothy with teaching and solid Apostolic guidance so he can go forward and teach God's word with confidence in order to settle the disruption caused by the promoters of this heretical doctrine.

2.
PAUL'S CHARGE TO TIMOTHY

I Timothy 1:1-11

We've reviewed the background of Paul's first letter to Timothy who was a young preacher working at the church in Ephesus which seemed to be embroiled in controversy over heretical teachers promoting "Gnostic" ideas. Gnosticism was a mixture of concepts and practices taken from philosophy, pagan mysticism, Judaism and Christianity which were brought together to form a new, and as some thought, superior form of doctrine replacing the gospel which Paul had originally taught these brethren.

Paul writes to Timothy with his own mix of encouragement, challenge and teaching in order to help him confront these false teachers, organize the church and prepare it for service in peaceful harmony.

Greetings (1:1-2)

> [1] Paul, an apostle of Christ Jesus according to the commandment of God our Savior, and of Christ Jesus, who is our hope, [2] To Timothy, my true child in the faith: Grace, mercy and peace from God the Father and Christ Jesus our Lord.

Vs. 1 - Paul introduces himself as an Apostle of Jesus, in the circle of the 12, by the command of both God and Jesus. This establishes his authority, his teachings and the source of both. Very early in the letter he introduces the idea that Christ is our hope, worthy of our trust (as opposed to trusting in some sort of secret knowledge or teachers).

Vs. 2 - He establishes the credibility and integrity of Timothy, the recipient of the letter whom Paul blesses. The idea of a "true child" not only denotes their closeness but also the fact that Timothy was trusted to represent Paul in spiritual matters as well. The blessing that he gives includes:

- **Grace** – favor or good things like past forgiveness and a future hope of heaven.
- **Mercy** – pity, help, compassion.
- **Peace** – harmony between God and man, as well as peace between men themselves.

With his opening lines Paul does the following:

- Declares his own inspired authority which is derived from God Himself.
- Confirms Timothy's charge to teach.
- Offers a blessing on the evangelist and the ministry he must fulfill at Ephesus.

This letter has the same charge to preachers today, giving them the same authority to instruct, correct and build up the church as it did for Timothy when it was first sent to him.

Paul and Timothy (1:3-20)

Paul's Charge to Timothy

Paul now turns to address Timothy directly and charge (challenge) him concerning the carrying out of his ministry, especially concerning the false doctrine being taught at Ephesus.

> [3] As I urged you upon my departure for Macedonia, remain on at Ephesus so that you may instruct certain men not to teach strange doctrines,

Timothy is reminded of his original charge to instruct certain men not to teach other doctrines (than had been taught by the Apostles). Some (Gnostic teachers) were straying from the teachings of Christ and the Apostles, and Timothy was to rebuke them for this and demand that they stop spreading their false ideas.

> [4] nor to pay attention to myths and endless genealogies, which give rise to mere speculation rather than furthering the administration of God which is by faith.

He gives a brief description of the type of teaching not to listen to and reminds Timothy that godly teaching is restricted to matters that develop faith and knowledge of God's word.

Paul makes a brief reference about myths and endless genealogies. These Jewish myths were not part of the inspired

Scriptures but rather a kind of speculation regarding genealogies found in Gnostic genealogical tables. These discussions did not produce the spiritual virtues that Paul mentions in the following verse:

> [5] But the goal of our instruction is love from a pure heart and a good conscience and a sincere faith.

The 'acid' test for the teaching of true and godly doctrine was the development of love as a direct result of that teaching. The 'fruit' of proper teaching from true teachers, Paul says, will be:

1. **Pure heart** – A clear mind and unwavering heart.
2. **Good conscience** – One whose conscience is clear because of trust in God's grace and a righteous lifestyle.
3. **Sincere faith** – A solid faith and assurance nourished by God's word, not secret knowledge.

Debates, pride and division are not the fruit of solid teaching from approved teachers.

> [6] For some men, straying from these things, have turned aside to fruitless discussion,

Some teachers who were on the right path have been distracted, Paul says, and have been caught up in this false teaching. They have "turned aside" means that they have left Christ's teaching in order to champion this new knowledge which Paul says is simply a waste of time.

> [7] wanting to be teachers of the Law, even though they do not understand either what they are saying or the matters about which they make confident assertions.

It seems that the Gnostic teachers' desire was to become something other than "Christ-like." The "Teachers of the Law" refers to rabbis of the Jewish religion. The Gnostic teachers wanted to assume this type of position and thus create a role of authority for themselves within the church. "Teachers of the Law" were not the same as Judaizers or the Circumcision Party who taught that you had to become a Jew and therefore be circumcised before you could become a Christian. This teaching was contrary to what Jesus required and taught by the Apostles (Matthew 28:18-20, Mark 16:15-16).

"Teachers of the Law" in this case referred to those at Philippi who were using certain ascetic practices found in the Jewish Law such as food or marriage restrictions as part of their Gnostic doctrines over which they became the teachers, arbitrators or "Christian" rabbis.

> [8] But we know that the Law is good, if one uses it lawfully,

Paul, the former Pharisee and expert in these matters, explains that the Law was given for specific purposes but in certain cases could be used incorrectly. These Gnostic teachers had formulated a new doctrine which was foreign to apostolic teaching in that they were binding certain aspects of the Law on Christians, and this was incorrect.

> [9a] realizing the fact that law is not made for a righteous person,

Paul, therefore, goes on to explain some of the proper uses for the Law (i.e. Ten Commandments and the ordinances contained in the Old Testament).

1. To reveal the nature of sin (Romans 3:20b; 7:7)
2. To reveal the punishment for sin (Romans 6:23)

3. To reveal God's justice (obey - live, disobey - die).

The Law was never given as a means to justify oneself before God; it was designed to reveal our unrighteousness and our need for God's forgiveness and mercy.

> [9b] but for those who are lawless and rebellious, for the ungodly and sinners, for the unholy and profane, for those who kill their fathers or mothers, for murderers [10a] and immoral men and homosexuals and kidnappers and liars and perjurers,

Paul continues to show that the Law is not directed at those who are saved. Christians are under the principle of grace, not the principle of law.

- Under the principle of grace God repeatedly forgives our sins, bears with our weaknesses, promises to transform us into perfect spiritual beings at the resurrection, and asks that we trust in Christ and remain faithful unto death.
- Under the principle of law if you sin once, you are condemned. Anything less than perfection is unacceptable. You are saved and receive glory only if you do not sin.

Paul, therefore, emphasizes the fact that Christians are not under law because the Law is designed for godless, unrepentant, ignorant sinners. He then goes on to give examples of the type of people that the Law will judge:

- **Lawless** – those who know the Law but act without concern for it.
- **Disobedient** – rebellious individuals, spoiled, undisciplined. Those who refuse to obey the Law.
- **Ungodly** – those who are irreverent, impious and without respect for spiritual things.

- **Sinners** – wicked, evil and immoral.
- **Unholy** – totally devoted to the world.
- **Profane** – those who ridicule spiritual or holy things.
- **Murderers of parents** – self-explanatory.
- **Man slayers** – aggressive, violent, unkind, oppressors.
- **Immoral persons** – all kinds of sexual sins.
- **Sodomites** – translated into English as homosexuals but the Bible has no word for homosexual therefore it simply describes the actions involved in these unions.
- **Kidnappers** – slave traders.
- **Liars** – hypocrites, dishonest (I John 2:4; 4:20).
- **Perjurers** – being false with the intent to injure someone else; not keeping vows.

This is not a complete list of sins but rather a representation of the kinds of people and sins that the Law will reveal, condemn, judge and then punish.

> [10b] and whatever else is contrary to sound teaching, [11] according to the glorious gospel of the blessed God, with which I have been entrusted

Paul completes this section by saying that aside from this list of sins, God will condemn and punish those who teach anything else other than the gospel given by Christ and taught by the Apostles.

The point he makes here is that any system of philosophy or religion which promotes another way to come into communion with God, other than salvation obtained through faith in Jesus Christ, will be judged/condemned and punished under the Law as something sinful.

Paul, in his charge to Timothy, confirms the idea that only the gospel, given by God to Christ who then taught it to the Apostles, is valid teaching. In saying this Paul makes two important points:

1. He establishes Timothy and his teachings as legitimately coming from God.
2. He condemns the teachings and teachers of Gnostic ideas as false.

Lessons

1. Nothing changes

2000 years after this letter was written the sins are exactly the same, the punishment is exactly the same and the way of salvation is exactly the same. However, there continues to be various solutions to the sin problem offered today that still keep God and the cross of Christ out of the equation.

2. The gospel is our only response

> I'm not ashamed of the gospel for it's the power of God unto salvation.
> - Romans 1:16

There are many young Timothys in today's generation who are insecure in their faith thinking that they are no match for the slick atheists of our time or the apologists who embrace a universal spirituality with no reference to Christ. There is, however, nothing new here or changed since the beginning. We still have the same cast of sinners, unbelievers and religious frauds who promise heaven without the cross of Christ and lead the ignorant into greater darkness.

We don't need to prove anything to atheists or disprove anything to those who have another religion. Our task, like

Timothy's, is to simply proclaim the gospel and live our lives faithfully in order to confirm that we actually believe what we preach.

The temptation to out-smart or out-debate atheists or to deconstruct everyone else's ideas about religion or spirituality are the devil's way of immobilizing us with the fear of ridicule and self-doubt.

We've been sent to proclaim and explain our faith, not other people's ideas about religion. Paul wasn't ashamed because he knew that the gospel message itself had the innate power to reach everyone from the pious Jew to the most worldly Gentile.

As Christians we have only one response to questions, challenges and ridicule, and that is the simple message of the gospel proclaimed in love. If we have answered in this way, we have fulfilled the charge given to us by Christ to preach the gospel to all nations (Matthew 28:18-20).

3.
PAUL'S PERSONAL WITNESS

I Timothy 1:12-20

In verses 1-11 of the opening chapter, Paul sets out to accomplish two important things to help Timothy deal with the issues he faced at Ephesus:

1. He establishes Timothy as a legitimate teacher who was teaching sound doctrine. Timothy was a young preacher facing difficult opponents in the church and Paul wanted to strengthen his position by giving him the benefit of his own apostolic approval.

2. Paul also condemned the doctrines of the Gnostic philosophers because they strayed from the original teachings of Jesus and the Apostles.

In this way the Apostle drew a "line" in the sand about who was approved as a teacher and which teachings were acceptable. Once done, Paul changes directions and offers a short prayer of thanksgiving before going on to address other matters.

Paul's Prayer of Thanksgiving — 1:12-17

Paul gives thanks to God, not only for giving him the ministry of apostleship (which he felt he didn't deserve since he was a persecutor of the church before being converted), but also for enabling him to actually do the difficult work required of a called Apostle. He was grateful to be chosen to serve God, and thankful for having successfully and dynamically done so for many years.

> [12] I thank Christ Jesus our Lord, who has strengthened me, because He considered me faithful, putting me into service,

Paul's ministry came from Christ who originally called and sustained the Apostle through his many trials. The false teachers were claiming some kind of authority based on their knowledge of secret information. Paul contrasted this by explaining the nature of his relationship and knowledge of Christ who authorized and supported him in ministry. He provides Timothy with this information in the context of a prayer.

> [13] even though I was formerly a blasphemer and a persecutor and a violent aggressor. Yet I was shown mercy because I acted ignorantly in unbelief; [14] and the grace of our Lord was more than abundant, with the faith and love which are found in Christ Jesus.

Paul's main point is that he did not deserve to be an Apostle because of who he was before God called him into ministry. He was a:

1. **Blasphemer** – As a Pharisee he denounced Christ as a fake and a troublemaker.
2. **Persecutor** – He was a persecutor of Christians who tortured and jailed many of them.

3. **Violent aggressor** – He was insolent, aggressive and angry with Jesus and His people.

This is who he was when he met Christ, and why, he says, he was unworthy to be a leader in the church.

Despite all of this, however, God had mercy on him because he did these things in ignorance of Christ. Even though he was ignorant and trying to please God in his own way, he was still sinning.

God showed him mercy by sending someone to preach the gospel to him (not by simply accepting his zeal or sincerity). Sincerity and zeal do not wash away our sins. These are washed away by the blood of Christ in the waters of baptism. We see in Acts 22:16 that Paul obeyed the gospel, reluctantly preached to him by Ananias, a servant of the Lord sent to Paul for this specific purpose.

God's love and mercy was shown to Paul in several ways:

1. Christ came to die for his sins.
2. God kept him alive to show him the ministry and blessings that would be given to him.
3. God gave him the ministry of announcing this good news to the Gentile world.

This grace, offered and received, was sufficient to save him and reset the course of his life (what is unsaid here is that he didn't need secret or special knowledge to gain these things).

> [15] It is a trustworthy statement, deserving full acceptance, that Christ Jesus came into the world to save sinners, among whom I am foremost of all.

Paul quotes one of the many "sayings" that were circulating in the church at the time. Today we say things like "What would Jesus do? Or, It's a God-thing!" These are phrases that express truths contained in God's word. In the same way, one of the sayings of that time was, "Christ came into the world to save sinners." Paul quotes the saying and confirms it as true when he compares it with his own life. In other words, his life is a prime example of this saying!

> [16] Yet for this reason I found mercy, so that in me as the foremost, Jesus Christ might demonstrate His perfect patience as an example for those who would believe in Him for eternal life.

Not only is this saying true, and true about him in particular, Paul says that he should be the "poster boy" for this saying so others like him could have confidence in God. The idea is that if God can forgive me, the chief sinner (who tried to destroy both the work and the people of God), then He can forgive anybody.

> [17] Now to the King eternal, immortal, invisible, the only God, be honor and glory forever and ever. Amen.

Verse 17 is a doxology (spontaneous praise). Here Paul is so overwhelmed with thanksgiving that he breaks into spontaneous praise to God. He says very specific things that we believe God to be:

- God is **eternal** – without beginning or end (I Timothy 6:16).
- God is **immortal** – not subject to decay (I Timothy 6:15).
- God is **invisible** – spiritual (John 4:24; Romans 1:20).

Such a being deserves honor and glory forever. Why? Because no one else is or has done these kinds of things for which they are being honored through praise. Have you never said in your prayers, "Only you, Lord, are worthy of praise!"

Paul's Charge to Timothy – 1:18-20

In the last part of this chapter, Paul renews his charge to Timothy.

> [18] This command I entrust to you, Timothy, my son, in accordance with the prophecies previously made concerning you, that by them you fight the good fight,

The charge or mission originally given to Timothy was based on what the Holy Spirit said about him through the prophets in the church. In the early church those with the gift of prophecy served to guide the church until the New Testament canon was recorded, collected and eventually distributed (Ephesians 4:11-12).

Paul reminds Timothy that since he was chosen in this way he should have confidence to enter into the battle against the false teachers. If God chose him for ministry, God would also be with him in ministry (Matthew 28:20).

> [19a] keeping faith and a good conscience.

Paul now explains the strategy needed in order to "fight the good fight" in the name of the Lord:

A. **Keep the faith** – Maintain or preserve the faith (the teachings of Christ). Keep preaching and arguing for Christ-centered doctrines. Keep believing these and encourage others to do so as well.

B. **Keep a good conscience** – Faith and moral standards go together. You can't remain faithful or be effective in helping others to remain faithful if your own moral life isn't good. Peter says that we need to "add to our faith moral excellence" (II Peter 1:5). Many times false doctrine or falling away from Christ is preceded by a moral decline.

> [19b] which some have rejected and suffered shipwreck in regard to their faith. [20] Among these are Hymenaeus and Alexander, whom I have handed over to Satan, so that they will be taught not to blaspheme.

Paul gives an example of those in the church who had rejected these principles and ruined their faith as a consequence. He mentions two men, Hymenaeus who is described in II Timothy 2:17 and his brother Alexander (not the blacksmith in II Timothy 4:14).

Paul declares that they were delivered to Satan, which is a figurative way of saying that they were disciplined. We use figurative terms like these today as well:

- "I took a beating on the stock market" doesn't mean that you were physically beaten.
- "My computer crashed" doesn't mean that it actually hit the floor and broke (although, that might be what you'd like to do to it at times).

There are many reasons and ways to "discipline" people in the church. For example:

1. **Public immorality**
    1. Sin - Incest/fornication - I Corinthians 5:1-5
    2. Discipline - Withdraw fellowship - I Corinthians 5:2;5

2. **Heresy / causing division**
    1. Sin - Creating division in the church - Romans 16:17
    2. Discipline - Withdraw fellowship
3. **Idleness / gossip**
    1. Sin - People not working (on purpose) and meddling in other's lives - II Thessalonians 3:10-15
    2. Discipline - Withdraw fellowship
4. **Disobedience**
    1. Sin - Will not obey the Scriptures or leadership - II Thessalonians 3:6
    2. Discipline - Withdraw fellowship
5. **Party spirit**
    1. Sin - Competition for leadership in the church - Titus 3:10
    2. Discipline - Withdraw fellowship after two warnings
6. **Personal sin / conflict**
    1. Sin - Personal offense Matthew 18:5-ff
    2. Discipline - Warn three times/withdraw fellowship

In the case of these two brothers who blasphemed (spoke with disrespect concerning God or sacred things) their core sin was that they promoted false doctrine over the gospel. Being turned over to Satan or being disciplined likely meant that they were withdrawn from or disfellowshipped (two terms used to describe church discipline). To be disfellowshipped means that you cannot enjoy fellowship with other Christians. For example, you are denied the blessing of hearing God's word at the public assembly, sharing communion or participating in other occasions, worship or social interaction with other believers. Jesus said that you are either with Him or with Satan. If, therefore, you are separated from Christians, you are also separated from Christ and thus associated with Satan. There is no third choice.

And so, Paul continues his encouragement of Timothy:

1. He encourages him to fight the battle with confidence because he's been called and equipped by God for this struggle. It was important for Timothy to keep this in mind since the ones who had the secret knowledge also assumed that they had a superior intellect.

2. He demonstrates that sometimes punishment is necessary for the good of the brethren, and provides examples to show how this should be carried out.

4.
PAUL'S INSTRUCTIONS ON PRAYER AND THE ROLE OF MEN AND WOMEN IN THE CHURCH

I Timothy 2:1-15

In chapter two of this letter, Paul will move from personal encouragement of Timothy, by confirming his teaching and the necessity of disciplining false teachers, to instructions concerning prayer and its purposes.

In this section, Paul will remind Timothy that prayers are to be made for all men so that mankind might come to know the truth and be saved. For this reason, Paul stresses that prayer is an absolute necessity in the work of bringing the lost to salvation. In addition to this, he also comments on the proper role of men and women in the church who are committed to the task of bringing the gospel to the world.

Instructions on Prayer – 2:1-7

Types of prayer

> First of all, then, I urge that entreaties and prayers, petitions and thanksgivings,
> - I Timothy 2:1a

Paul describes different types of prayers and objectives we should strive for in our conversations with God.

A. Supplication (entreaties)

This means a specific request or a request within a certain situation. For example, "Dear God, please help my husband to find a job."

B. Prayer

A general word referring to all types of prayers that we make throughout our day (e.g. request, adoration, praise, confession, etc.).

Note the difference between supplication and prayer: we should always pray that our families be saved; a supplication, however, takes place when we pray that our cousin, who has begun to study the Bible, obey the gospel. Supplications are more specific.

C. Intercession (Petition)

This word suggests a more intimate relationship with God. It is a pleading or a begging of God, without restraint, on someone else's behalf. In Romans 8:27, 34, Paul says that the Spirit and Jesus do this for Christians. We can intercede for others with God because the Spirit is within us (Acts 2:38) and Christ is among us (Matthew 28:20).

D. Thanksgiving

Gratitude is the first of the heavenly virtues. Ingratitude, on the other hand, is the first step that leads to total ungodliness (Romans 1:21). Cultivating a grateful attitude in prayer and in life leads us to a more peaceful heart and joyful spirit. Gratitude for what God provides enables us to enjoy our blessings without guilt.

Who to Pray for

> [1b] ...be made on behalf of all men, [2] for kings and all who are in authority, so that we may lead a tranquil and quiet life in all godliness and dignity.
> - I Timothy 2:1b-2

Prayer for all because salvation for all begins with prayer. Even those in authority, kings and rulers, are to be subjects of our prayers. At that time, there was an issue in the church where some felt that it was not right to pray for pagan rulers. Paul, however, teaches them that when society is at peace and running well, it is easier to proclaim the gospel and for this reason it is necessary to pray for those whose charge it is to maintain that social order.

- Tranquil and quiet - A calm and orderly nation without strife describes the priority task of rulers in society, this and to maintain justice as well.

- Godliness and dignity - These words describe a Christian's state of mind in an environment of quietness and tranquility. Godliness means that one is devoted to God. Dignity describes one who is serious or sober-minded.

Although these attributes are best developed in times of peace, they can also be cultivated in times of stress and war.

Why should we pray for these things? (verses 3-7)

A. This is God's will

> [3] This is good and acceptable in the sight of God our Savior, [4] who desires all men to be saved and to come to the knowledge of the truth.
> - I Timothy 2:3-4

God is pleased when this environment is present. These prayers are offered, therefore, because they promote His ultimate goal, which is the saving of all men. God wants everyone to know the truth and to be saved, not just a chosen few, and this is best achieved in a society that is orderly and at peace.

B. God's will is worked out with the gospel

> [5] For there is one God, and one mediator also between God and men, the man Christ Jesus, [6] who gave Himself as a ransom for all, the testimony given at the proper time. [7] For this I was appointed a preacher and an apostle (I am telling the truth; I am not lying) as a teacher of the Gentiles in faith and truth.
> - I Timothy 2:5-7

There is only one God and one manner in which men can be saved (through the preaching of the gospel), therefore, any environment that promotes or facilitates this activity is pleasing to God. In verse 6 Paul makes a parenthetical statement reviewing the main points of the gospel message (Christ's atoning death to redeem or to pay for our sins).

Since this letter was designed to ultimately serve the church at large, its contents were meant to be taught publicly. Paul, therefore, takes this opportunity to mention the gospel in general terms and uses the word ransom (ransom for all). A ransom is a payment made to buy something back. In this sense, Jesus is the ransom given to buy back our moral debts owed to God and thus free us from the penalty of death at judgment due to our sins.

This, not the Gnostic teachers' ideas, was the true gospel and manner of salvation. The testimony, given at the proper time, refers to the many who had proclaimed this message throughout history:

- Mankind's salvation to come, spoken of by the prophets.
- God announcing Christ's deity and work to the Apostles:
  - at His baptism
  - at the Mount of Transfiguration
  - at His resurrection
- The proclamation of the gospel by the Apostles at Pentecost
  - God declared His plan to save man at proper times and events throughout history so that everyone could receive the good news.
- Paul concludes that he has been chosen to be one of these proclaimers (in a long line of proclaimers) about the manner in which God would save mankind.
  - This is why he says that he was chosen to be a preacher, a proclaimer and an Apostle (special messenger).
  - His particular mission was to bring the message of the gospel to the non-Jews (Gentiles).

Unlike the Gnostic teachers, he does not lie but always teaches the truth faithfully. This truth that he proclaims to the Gentiles is that we are saved by God's grace through faith in Jesus Christ.

Instructions on Conduct and Role – 2:8-15

A. Men

> Therefore I want the men in every place to pray, lifting up holy hands, without wrath and dissension.
> - I Timothy 2:8

Verse 8 summarizes and climaxes verses 1-7.

Since God wants all to live in quietness and security so that the saving gospel can be preached, we should be busy making all kinds of prayers for people in power, like kings and others in positions of influence.

With this in mind, Paul specifies that he wants men (the word is not generic. It is not mankind, or humans. The Greek word is for a male, actually for a husband) to lead the prayer. When the types of prayers he mentions in the first chapter are prayed, the men are the ones who should be doing the praying.

"In every place" refers to every place where public worship is offered; since this letter is an instruction to the church, not to the family unit, and is meant to direct the ministers in how to conduct church affairs, especially when it gathers publicly.

Paul also specifies that those who pray are not to be just any male, but the ones that are qualified: only those men who could lift up holy hands (lifting hands was the Jewish style of prayer, a different posture than today). Paul is more concerned with the man's character than the style of his posture in prayer.

The term holy refers to a person who is pure and undefiled, who is clean. How could an immoral brother's prayer be effective on behalf of another, without wrath or dissension? This description refers to one who is not a cause of trouble or division in the church. Men who lead in prayer have the responsibility to remain pure and peaceful. Better to have no prayer than a prayer by one who is not qualified.

The man that prays brings all of the hopes and needs of the church before God in prayer. He, therefore, should be worthy and prepared to go before the King of glory!

Culture vs. Command

This verse concerning prayer and who is to lead it brings up a common point of discussion, and sometimes division, in the assembly: the role of women in the church.

There are various opinions on this issue. Here are four main positions:

1. **The conservative view.** Brethren who hold this opinion teach that women should do nothing in public worship, except sit and listen, both during the worship and the Bible class. Women never speak, period.
2. **The mainline position**. Here, Christian women help, perhaps by preparing the elements for the communion. They do participate in Bible class and share their ideas but they do not teach a mixed class of adults (male-female) and do not preach during the worship assembly.
3. **The progressive view**. These brethren encourage women to participate in the public assembly by passing the communion trays, leading prayer, and they believe that woman can serve as deacons (deaconess).
4. **The liberal view.** In short, women and men can do all of the ministries, including serving as elders, deacons or preachers.

The differences in positions are caused by a disagreement over the concepts of culture and command. In other words, what belongs to culture and can be changed as culture evolves, and what belongs to Divine commands, which are given by God and not subject to change. Deciding which parts and activities in the church belong to either cultural mores or Divine commands cause the differences that exist between various groups and thus create division.

A. A modern example of changing culture in the church - dress codes: Today, many women wear jeans to church. One hundred years ago, however, a woman wearing pants to church, let alone jeans, would have been scandalous. Today, however, in our culture, we think nothing of it. This practice is part of evolving culture and the church has to adapt as things like this change.

B. An ancient example of changing culture in the church - foot washing: While sharing the Passover meal with them, Jesus told His Apostles to wash each other's feet (John 13:5-15). While actually washing their feet that night He said to them, *"If I, your teacher, wash your feet, you should wash each other's feet."*

Does this, therefore, mean that every time we have communion we should wash each other's feet? In answering this question we must first understand that in that time and culture, foot washing was a sign of hospitality and respect. Those walking on dusty roads wearing sandals were welcomed into a home with the opportunity to bathe their dirty and tired feet before entering their host's home.

- Today, we have cars, shoes, carpets and slippers. The cultural ritual of foot washing is gone, but the meaning behind it remains. Today, we do other things to show our love, welcome, respect and humility before others. For example, we offer our own room to sleep in for overnight guests or we give them a favorite comfortable place to sit while they visit and offer them their preferred refreshments.

Jesus taught His Apostles to humble themselves, to respect others and to offer hospitality. He used a cultural form of that era, foot washing, to make His point.

- The Apostles continued to teach the church to humble itself, as well as love and respect others. Paul taught this in Ephesians 4:31-5:2 and John did so in I John 4:7. But they did not command foot washing as the way to demonstrate this Christian humility, respect and love. It was an eternal principle wrapped in the first-century custom of foot washing.

We have other ways and cultural forms today that enable us to practice the eternal principle of love and hospitality.

C. An ancient example of Divine command - baptism: Jesus commanded His disciples to be baptized as their response of faith to the gospel (Matthew 28:18-20, Mark 16:16). At that time, baptism (immersion in water) was an ancient religious cultural form used by both pagans and Jews, usually as a purification rite.

Jesus took this form and gave it His meaning (regeneration). He tied this practice to the gospel message and commanded the Apostles to preach this to the world (Matthew 28:18-20; Mark 16:15-16). The Apostles taught and preserved this rite in their writings. They commanded that it remain unchanged as part of the gospel message (Galatians 3:26-28). This was a religious and cultural form that was given by Jesus to keep, and confirmed by the Apostles' teaching (Acts 2:38; 22:16). Baptism was and continues to be an enduring command and remains despite the changes in culture since it was introduced because:

- Jesus commanded it.
- He imposed it upon all those who would become His disciples.
- The Apostles taught and preserved this rite in their sacred writings.

- They taught other Christians and preached to non-Christians that baptism was a necessary step in the process of becoming a Christian.
- This remains a command today and is meant to be kept until Jesus returns (Ephesians 4:5).

Many issues of disagreement, therefore, between liberals and conservatives crop up when determining what is a command and thus not changeable, and what is subject to the natural changes that can be made when things are in the area of man-made customs and cultural practices. Churches, therefore, that have women who serve as deacons or practicing homosexuals who serve as ministers do so because they consider certain issues simply cultural things that can be changed to suit today's mindset. For example, those who use the "cultural" argument to defend their practices claim that homosexuality was forbidden in the first-century simply because it was not accepted in Jewish culture (of course this was so because it was forbidden in Scripture - Leviticus 18:22). Their conclusion is that today we are more permissive of this in our culture, so it has become acceptable in churches as well.

The key is to realize that some things in the Bible <u>are</u> based on culture and subject to change, and some are eternal commands and not to be changed ever. The goal is being able to know the difference and being gracious with those who disagree.

The point of all this is as follows, in this epistle Paul specifically calls on the men to pray in every place. Was this instruction given based on culture or command? One could legitimately make the argument that it was a cultural norm for men to be in leadership roles at that time, especially in Jewish society. However, it was also true that women served in pagan temples, taking significant leadership roles in Greek and Roman religious rites.

The answer lies in noting that Paul is teaching this to the church as a general instruction, and this instruction is confirmed in another passage with even stronger language.

> [34] The women are to keep silent in the churches; for they are not permitted to speak, but are to subject themselves, just as the Law also says.
> [35] If they desire to learn anything, let them ask their own husbands at home; for it is improper for a woman to speak in church. [36] Was it from you that the word of God first went forth? Or has it come to you only?
> [37] If anyone thinks he is a prophet or spiritual, let him recognize that the things which I write to you are the Lord's commandment.
> - I Corinthians 14:34-37

Paul was giving a command for the entire church and had the right to do so because the Lord had authorized him as a chosen Apostle (Romans 1:1) to teach this concerning men and women's roles in the assembly.

Also, there is no other teaching that contradicts this anywhere in the New Testament. This practice was universally followed in the early church when it gathered for public worship. That holy and peace-loving Christian men were to lead in prayer whenever the church met for public worship was what Paul taught and the only teaching provided on this matter in the New Testament.

It may be tempting to change this in light of different attitudes about women in our culture today. However, we have to remember that our first goal is not to follow the fashion of today's culture but to remain faithful to the teachings of God's word.

Our task is to know what God desires and carefully follow that, even when it is not popular.

B. Women

Paul explains how men are to express godliness (holy hands, etc.). Now, he explains how women are to do the very same thing.

> [9] Likewise, I want women to adorn themselves with proper clothing, modestly and discreetly, not with braided hair and gold or pearls or costly garments, [10] but rather by means of good works, as is proper for women making a claim to godliness.
> - I Timothy 2:9-10

Note that he says "likewise." In the same manner that the men are to comply to God's will, so are the women. He teaches that the women who claim to be godly need to practice or avoid certain things. Of course, the things a woman does in order to be godly are the same today as they were then. Jesus charged men with certain things to do that do not change. The same thing can be said of women. Both men and women do similar things today to achieve this state. Being honest, kind and righteous are things that have no gender. This epistle, therefore, applies to women of the first century in the same way that it does to women of our day.

Two thousand years ago, therefore, Paul said that if women wanted to be seen as "righteous" there were some things that they needed to do:

- **Adorn -** They needed to cover and surround themselves with things that were good and godly.
- **Proper clothing -** The word proper, here, provides the context for this teaching. Clothing that was proper for the gathering of the saints at that time. Proper in the sense that the clothing was indicative and reflective of other religious and holy women of the era.

This is where the wearing of a veil by a Christian woman became an issue. In first century culture the veil meant that a woman was self-controlled and respected the leadership of her father or her husband. Without the veil a woman could not freely and easily move about in that society. At that time, veils were the proper way to express this truth. Today, however, they do not represent this. On the contrary, if a woman wears a veil today she is actually separating herself from the culture (in non-Muslim societies).

The covering of oneself also pointed to one's attitude of modesty. It was the clothing and the attitude together that mirrored a person's true character. Paul describes the proper attitude and behavior that a Christian woman should cultivate then as well as now. For example:

- Purity and decency, as opposed to suggestive or sensual – A woman who reveals her body in some immodest way reveals her lack of love for her Christian brothers, who may have to struggle with lust and other sins, provoked by her immodesty and their weaknesses. After all, love is kind (I Corinthians 13:4).
- Modesty also refers to a freedom from conceit, pride or vanity – Many women spend more time preparing the outside before coming to worship, but very little time preparing the inside.

Paul links the word "discreetly" to the word "modesty." The word discreet does not simply mean that a person can keep a secret:

- It means to be sober or serious-minded or spiritually-minded.
- Not given to showing off, not ostentatious, frivolous or silly.
- Not overdressed to create a false or puffed up attitude.

- Also, not under-dressed to create a false image of poverty, or not caring about one's appearance.
- It means to be mature and reflect that maturity in how one dresses, lives and relates to others, as well as how we use our resources.

Paul says that the way to adorn or cover ourselves with modesty and discretion is not by wearing certain clothing or jewelry, or the way the hair is fixed. It seemed that in the church at that time there was an attempt by women to make statements about their position in society by what they wore and how their hair was done (note that nothing has changed).

Paul is not saying that a woman cannot look well groomed, wear jewelry or have her hair done. He is merely saying that these are not the things that create a sense of modesty and discretion in a Christian woman. He also says that a woman achieves true modesty and discretion by covering herself with good deeds. Jewels, fashionable clothing, makeup and hair are not wrong in themselves (with God, all these things are neutral). However, if a woman depends on these things to please God or to be noticed by Him, she will be disappointed in the end.

The point is that God notices and blesses obedient, humble, godly and modest men and women in the church.

Attitude of Women While Learning

Paul leaves off the idea of how a woman needs to be – pleasing to God, and moves on to the issue of how women should conduct themselves while learning and worshiping in the assembly which, he has previously taught, needs to be led by men.

> A woman must quietly receive instructions with entire submissiveness.
> - I Timothy 2:11

Quiet

Here, the word quiet (Greek - HÉSUCHIA) refers to one's quiet disposition or tranquil nature, which is a manifestation of a meek and gentle inner life.

It is an attitude of mind and does not mean to keep absolute silence, otherwise how could a woman sing praises to God, confess Christ or proclaim the amen! It is the ability to learn in a spirit that does not disturb others. Just because a person does not teach or lead, or says little in class, does not mean that they are quietly receiving instruction. Quietly receiving instruction is learning in the spirit of gentleness and humility. This spirit will be evident even in a woman who asks questions.

Submissive

Submissiveness is her outward attitude (quiet is the inward attitude). In these circumstances, it would mean that she neither takes on the role of teacher nor judges the teacher. Submissive, as a student, is to learn what is being taught with a mind to apply something to one's life, rather than listening to the lesson and judging the ability of the teacher and his knowledge.

The point is that a woman is to cultivate an attitude which promotes personal growth and knowledge within her, and harmony with others around her.

> But I do not allow a woman to teach or exercise authority over a man, but to remain quiet.
> - I Timothy 2:12

Apposition

An apposition is a grammatical construction where two words refer to a common thing or person. For example, today I prayed to the Lord Jesus. In this sentence, Lord and Jesus are two words that refer to the same person. Paul uses this apposition device in verse 12 with the words *teach* and *authority*. In the Jewish culture, the one who taught was also the one who had the authority.

In regard to women, Paul is saying that a woman is not to exercise authority over a brother in the body of Christ when it meets. In the church, teaching and preaching involves the exercise of spiritual authority. It did then and it continues to do so now.

- When there is a mixed assembly, men are to provide the spiritual leadership embodied in the teacher's role.
- Women can teach, however. They can teach other women, they can share the gospel and teach the unsaved, they can teach children.

The Bible is silent on women's role in the world of professional employment. There is nothing in the Scriptures that says a woman cannot work outside the home. A woman can become President of the United States and due the respect and authority that is associated with that position to the same degree that it would if a man held that role, but in the church she receives instruction quietly (even if she served as President in the world of politics). This is her challenge in the modern world. Obeying God in this question, against all social norms in our culture, is very difficult. We should note that men also balked at Jesus' teaching, whether they were Jews or Gentiles, in that they did not like the fact that they were to only have one wife. However, if they were to be faithful disciples they had to submit to teachings that were a personal challenge and not only those that were easy and advantageous to accept (i.e. all sins forgiven).

Two Reasons Why the Teaching on the Role of the Women in the Church is a Command and Not a Cultural Thing.

> [13] For it was Adam who was first created, and then Eve. [14] And it was not Adam who was deceived, but the woman being deceived, fell into transgression.
> - I Timothy 2:13-14

According to Paul, this teaching is eternal and unchangeable for two reasons:

1. God Created Man First, and Then Woman - verse 13

Man has the primary position in the creation, established by God, not society. Paul confirms this idea in I Corinthians 11:2-3. In the spiritual body of Christ (the church) all things function according to the spiritual order and the divine model, not the secular model. The church is not like society, the government or corporations. It is a spiritual entity and it is organized along spiritual lines. There is God, Christ, man and then woman: this is the divine order and this order is reflected in the church.

2. Woman Sinned First - verse 14

Eve was deceived into disobedience. Adam was not fooled; he was induced through his feelings for his wife. Because of this deception God reestablished (originally Adam and Eve were co-rulers of the creation - Genesis 1:28) the role of the woman as one of submission to her husband (this done to establish peace and order in the home and society. Otherwise man would use his natural physical strength to impose a position of superiority and woman would use her natural complex psychological make-up to usurp man's attempt to dominate her thus creating a never ending struggle between the sexes that would result in chaos). The position of submission was assigned to her by God because she answered Satan's seduction. She was seduced into exchanging her allegiance with her husband for a partnership with Satan and brought her husband into that union which led to their downfall and the ruin of mankind after them.

Her original position of co-rulership was replaced with her new role as submissive wife and her punishment was to be the birthing of children in sorrow and pain. Giving birth to a child was meant to be a happy experience but turned into a sorrowful and painful one for her and all women in the future. This is the idea that helps explain verse 15.

> But women will be preserved through the bearing of children if they continue in faith and love and sanctity with self-restraint.
> - I Timothy 2:15

This experience of birthing and raising children, however, would be turned into a favorable one because of her ultimate salvation. If she continued in this universal life-giver role, and she did so with faith, love, purity, modesty and good sense, she would survive child bearing and rearing, and would also survive death to be raised again (along with her husband) to eternal life when Jesus returned.

Summary

Paul sets the initial structure of the church by ordering it along fundamental lines of men and women. He establishes what is natural and what is eternal, what is commanded as well as what is cultural, and the roles that men and women should play in the body of Christ.

In the following section of his letter, Paul will discuss the qualifications of those men who are responsible for the leadership in the local church.

5.
THE ROLE, WORK AND QUALIFICATIONS OF ELDERS

I Timothy 3:1-7

Now that Paul has taught on the subject of the proper role of men and women in the church, he goes on to describe the qualifications necessary for leadership in that same body. He begins by teaching that men, not women, are to aspire to spiritual leadership in the body of Christ and defines the character of those few who will fulfill that position in the assembly.

God has always provided leadership for His people, it is no different for the church today. Elders are those who lead the church and Paul will describe which men can aspire to this important role.

The preacher or evangelist's task is to recognize and develop potential leaders for the church. This is what Paul is teaching Timothy in this chapter: helping and guiding him in his search for and development of men who will eventually grow into church leaders.

The Meaning of the Terms Elder, Overseer and Pastor

> It is a trustworthy statement: if any man aspires to the office of overseer, it is a fine work he desires *to do*.
> - I Timothy 3:1

Paul begins by commending those who would seek leadership roles in the church. To have this desire is good, he says, and the position itself is a good thing to want.

- So many men feel unworthy, unprepared or too unspiritual to serve as leaders in the church.
- Paul addresses this issue immediately by stating that to want to serve in this way is not necessarily motivated by pride. It is a good and legitimate desire to want to lead God's people.

To "aspire" means to reach out for. It seems that the phrase he quotes, "if any man..." was a familiar saying in the early church. It was similar to modern expressions such as, "Praise the Lord" and Paul confirmed that the saying was true and accurate. Therefore, the first qualification of an elder was the desire to serve in this role. If a man had to be pressured, or if he served out of guilt or without conviction, he showed that he lacked the first and most important qualification for this task which was the actual desire to serve.

There are three Greek words used to describe the person and role of a church leader. All three words, however, describe the same person and the same role - just different facets of the man and his work.

1. PRESBUTEROS – Presbyter / Elder

- This term describes the type of man - a person of maturity.

- It refers to a man's age. One who is older than others by comparison (e.g. the elder brother in the parable of the prodigal son, Luke 15:25).
- It also indicates the office or position of elder - I Peter 5:5. The context determines the meaning, whether it is referring to one's maturity or office (position/role).
- The Jews used the term "PRESBUTEROS" to describe the older men as well as the office of elder within the synagogue and the Sanhedrin (ruling council) - Matthew 16:21.
- The Gentiles used this same word to describe a position within the local government of a city or town (i.e. the city elders).

Both Jews and Gentiles, therefore, were well aware of the significance of this word in reference to leadership as well as the maturity of the one who held this type of position.

2. EPISKOPOS – Overseer / Bishop / Superintendent / Guardian

- The term "EPISKOPOS" describes the work or office which the elder exercises.
- However, at times it refers to the person who actually does the work.
- It suggests authority - the authority to lead, oversee, supervise, guard. I Timothy 3:1 and Acts 20:28 use this word. I Peter 2:25 uses this term in reference to Jesus ("...guardian of your souls").

In Philippians 1:1, Paul demonstrates that this role of "overseer/bishop" was a specific office in the church and not simply a "leadership quality" of certain men in the congregation: *"To all the saints in Christ Jesus who are in Philippi, including the overseers and deacons..."*

3. POIMEN – Shepherd / Pastor

- This word describes the way the man actually did the work.
- The word describes the attitude that the leader has in his work with the congregation under his care (Matthew 9:36 - used for Christ; Ephesians 4:11 - pastor, one who shepherds).

It was the most familiar imagery of leadership for both Jews and Gentiles of that day: a shepherd caring for and guarding his flock.

Note that all three words apply and refer to the same person and office within the church. All English translations refer to the same person and thus the same role:

- Presbyter (the term priest comes from this word).
- Elder, overseer, bishop, superintendent, guardian, shepherd, pastor: In the Bible (New Testament) all of these words refer to the same person. For example, the same man can be a father, son, brother, husband and friend. These words can describe different aspects and relationships of the same man. In the same way, the New Testament writers used a variety of words to more fully describe the men who served as leaders in the church.

In the New Testament, this person was always a man and always served in a group of two or more men for each congregation (see Acts 14:23; 15:2; 15:23; 20:17; 28; Philippians 1:1; I Thessalonians 5:12; Hebrews 13:17; I Peter 5:5). In other words, churches described in the New Testament never had women as elders or pastors, and no church had only a single pastor or elder leading it (as we see today), they were always described as having two or more men who served as leaders in the local assembly.

Also, in the New Testament there was never a bishop/pastor/elder put in charge of more than one congregation. The idea of a pyramidic organization as we see in many modern religious denominations today was foreign to the New Testament image of the church. Each congregation in the New Testament had its own elders who led locally but had no authority beyond their local congregation.

The following verse is a good example of these words all being used in the same sentence :

> Be on guard for yourselves and for all the flock, among which the Holy Spirit has made you overseers, to shepherd the church of God which He purchased with His own blood.
> - Acts 20:28

- Paul has sent for the PRESBUTOROS (verse 17) to come to see him (the elders).
- In verse 28 he tells the EPISKOPOS (overseers/bishops/guardians) to POIMEN (shepherd) the flock which is the church.

Three different words to refer to the same group of men to do the same work. Mature men (elders) who had the responsibility and authority (bishops/overseers/guardians) to care for the church (shepherd/pastor).

The Work of Church Leaders

Before we go on to the following verses that describe the qualifications necessary for church leaders, we need to examine the work that leaders were called upon to perform.

1. Teach

> An overseer, then, must be above reproach, the husband of one wife, temperate, prudent, respectable, hospitable, able to teach,
> - I Timothy 3:2

Paul says "apt," meaning skilled for teaching. Skilled at giving or providing instruction to others.

Since the church grows by its knowledge of God's word in theory and practice, this ability is extremely important.

2. Protect

> Be on guard for yourselves and for all the flock, among which the Holy Spirit has made you overseers, to shepherd the church of God which He purchased with His own blood.
> - Acts 20:28

- Pastors have an attitude of watchfulness over the church.
- Bishops mainly watch and protect the church against false doctrines and practices that go against God's word.
- Titus 1:9 - An elder's method of defense is to know the Word himself and maintain sound doctrine in the face of opposition. As mentioned before, he must be able to refute false teaching if necessary.
- Hebrews 13:17 - Elders are watchmen, responsible for souls. Their task and appointment are from God so they must be careful in what they teach and how they live.

3. Lead

> The elders who rule well are to be considered worthy of double honor, especially those who work hard at preaching and teaching.
> - I Timothy 5:17

They stand before the congregation not as kings but as shepherds.

> [1] Therefore, I exhort the elders among you, as your fellow elder and witness of the sufferings of Christ, and a partaker also of the glory that is to be revealed, [2] shepherd the flock of God among you, exercising oversight not under compulsion, but voluntarily, according to the will of God; and not for sordid gain, but with eagerness; [3] nor yet as lording it over those allotted to your charge, but proving to be examples to the flock. [4] And when the Chief Shepherd appears, you will receive the unfading crown of glory.
> - I Peter 5:1-5

Elders lead in Christ-likeness. This means that their leadership is not only exercised over budget matters but also seen and felt in holiness, sacrifice, service, mercy and spiritual maturity. How else does the flock learn and imitate these things unless there are some who lead in them?

4. Pray and Minister to the Sick

> [14] Is anyone among you sick? Then he must call for the elders of the church and they are to pray over him, anointing him with oil in the name of the Lord; [15] and the prayer offered in faith will restore the one who is sick, and the Lord will raise him up, and if

> he has committed sins, they will be forgiven him.
> - James 5:14-15

We want the most mature spiritual members to pray and minister to us, and in most congregations these individuals are usually found among the elders.

James 5:14-15 could mean two things:

- A prayer of faith can raise up those suffering from various illnesses and injuries.
- A prayer of faith can strengthen someone who has been weakened by the ravages of sin.

Either meaning is possible based on the Greek words used in the passage. We can use the meaning that fits because both are true and can apply. For example:

- Acts 8:11-24 - Simon asked Peter to pray for his sin.
- Acts 28:8 - Prayer and the laying on of hands was done on behalf of someone who was physically ill.

Anointing with Oil

- Anointing with oil was a sacred custom among the Jews.
- Kings were anointed at coronation. This is how the term, "The Lord's anointed one" became synonymous with the term "king" (I Samuel 12:3-5).
- The Jews believed that the anointing with oil carried with it a transfer of holiness and virtue from the Lord in whose name the anointing was done.
- They also thought that it imparted a special blessing of the Spirit (I Samuel 16:12-13).
- In the same way that the faith of the individual being immersed was the active ingredient in the rite of baptism,

the anointing with oil was effective because of the faith involved and not because the oil itself had special power.

5. Shepherd the Flock

> [3] So He told them this parable, saying, [4] "What man among you, if he has a hundred sheep and has lost one of them, does not leave the ninety-nine in the open pasture and go after the one which is lost until he finds it? [5] When he has found it, he lays it on his shoulders, rejoicing. [6] And when he comes home, he calls together his friends and his neighbors, saying to them, 'Rejoice with me, for I have found my sheep which was lost!' [7] I tell you that in the same way, there will be more joy in heaven over one sinner who repents than over ninety-nine righteous persons who need no repentance.
> - Luke 15:3-7

The church leader models his role after Christ and thus becomes the source of protection, spiritual nourishment and guidance in the Christian way for the congregation. The "work of a shepherd" is what the qualifications in I Timothy 3:2-7 fit him for.

6. Discipline

> [9] holding fast the faithful word which is in accordance with the teaching, so that he will be able both to exhort in sound doctrine and to refute those who contradict.[10] For there are many rebellious men, empty talkers and deceivers, especially those of the circumcision, [11] who must be silenced because they are upsetting whole families, teaching things they should not teach for the sake of sordid gain.
> - Titus 1:9-11

Discipline means two things or activities:

1. To give teaching and correction to one who is in error (I Thessalonians 5:12-14).

2. To rebuke and admonish the disobedient, rebellious or divisive ones in the church (Titus 3:10; II Thessalonians 3:6, 14).

In every organization or family, someone needs to have the authority to protect against external attack or the danger of internal rebellion. The elders serve this purpose in the church.

7. Mature the Saints

> [11] And He gave some as apostles, and some as prophets, and some as evangelists, and some as pastors and teachers, [12] for the equipping of the saints for the work of service, to the building up of the body of Christ; [13] until we all attain to the unity of the faith, and of the knowledge of the Son of God, to a mature man, to the measure of the stature which belongs to the fullness of Christ. [14] As a result, we are no longer to be children, tossed here and there by waves and carried about by every wind of doctrine, by the trickery of men, by craftiness in deceitful scheming; [15] but speaking the truth in love, we are to grow up in all aspects into Him who is the head, even Christ, [16] from whom the whole body, being fitted and held together by what every joint supplies, according to the proper working of each individual part, causes the growth of the body for the building up of itself in love.
> - Ephesians 4:11-16

The elder's role is to help the church mature spiritually as it imitates and serves Jesus Christ, the head of the church. When Christ comes, He will complete the elders' task of transforming the church into what it was designed to be: the perfect body and complement to Christ Himself. For now, these men provide spiritual leadership through their teaching and example, and guide the church so its activities are in line with overall biblical principles.

Qualifications of Elders — I Timothy 3:2-7

> An overseer, then, must be above reproach, the husband of one wife, temperate, prudent, respectable, hospitable, able to teach,
> - I Timothy 3:2

1. Above Reproach

Paul begins with positive attributes.

- This term does not mean that this person is without sin but rather a man who has made right, to the best of his abilities, the things that are wrong in his life so that these matters cannot be charged to him again.
- He now lives in such a way that he will not cause shame on himself or the church.

2. The Husband of One Wife

There have been many debates about this verse and what it means. For example:

- A person who has only had one wife in all of his life and she is still alive.
- A person who is not a polygamist, although he may have been one in the past.

- A person who is properly married at present even though he may have been unmarried (i.e. widower or divorcee) in the past.

The literal translation of the saying "husband of one wife" is "a one-woman man." Paul could have said, "..a man who has never been divorced or widowed," in order to eliminate men with this type of marital history from being considered, but he chose this saying instead.

In my opinion, I believe that he was referring to this person's "attitude" and not to his "legal" status (i.e. widower, divorcee or remarried etc.). I do so because all of the other qualifications he mentions concerning this individual refer to his attitude and character. The term, "one-woman man" therefore, eliminates polygamists and also speaks to his faithfulness as a husband (whether widowed or divorced previously). In other words, not a flirt, not one who is improperly involved with other women even if he is married to only one. How a man conducts himself with women who are not his wife would seem to be a more relevant trait contributing to a man's work as an elder than whether or not he was a remarried widower or divorcee. I believe Paul's point is that a church leader is devoted to the woman he is married to, and other women not only respect that about him but feel safe when around him especially in situations when his wife is not present.

3. Temperate

- One who thinks straight, sober minded.
- A person who is not easily influenced by every new idea or carried away by emotion.
- Someone who is well balanced emotionally and not given to excesses in his appetites.

4. Prudent

- He has a balanced sense of judgment, is self-controlled and careful.
- Someone not swayed by sudden impulse.

5. Respectable

- Dignified (but not haughty or regal).
- He has inward moral excellence that shows itself in an outward orderly existence.
- His behavior is consistent and diligent.
- His conduct inspires respect from others.

6. Hospitable

- The word in the original Greek language, translated into the English word hospitable, meant "lover of strangers."
- In New Testament times, hospitality offered to preachers and teachers who traveled from place to place exercising their ministry was critical in the development and growth of the church. Hospitality was not simply a social grace, it was an important ministry that contributed directly to the growth of the assembly.
- This quality of character referred not only to the generous offering of food and lodging to strangers but also described a person who accepted those of different cultures, ideas and backgrounds with grace and kindness.

7. Apt to Teach

- The word refers to one who is skillful in teaching.
- A person who gets results and grows in his ability to teach others.
- It does not necessarily mean that one had to be an orator or academic to lead. Many simple men of limited education have a gift for communicating with others in a way that enables them to understand clearly the things of God.

> not addicted to wine or pugnacious, but gentle, peaceable, free from the love of money.
> - I Timothy 3:3

8. Not a Drunkard

This is where he begins the negative attributes.

- Wine was a common beverage (like water) in New Testament times, so the point was not to abstain from wine (which was widely used with meals).
- The passage means that an elder is not addicted to wine (or to any other thing for that matter - porn, video, etc.).

9. Not Pugnacious

- This term refers to a man who is a brawler, a fighter or is easily confrontational.
- Someone who is aggressive or verbally abusive cannot and should not lead in the church.

10. Gentle (Positive)

- One who is not self-willed (i.e. my way or the highway).
- A person who can be flexible, considerate of the views of others, yielding and not authoritarian. After all, church leadership is communal by design and requires those who can work with and through a group.

11. Peaceable

- Elders should not be quarrelsome by nature or known for causing strife and division. Some, through gossip or a combative attitude, cause trouble wherever they are.
- Elders bring and maintain peace and harmony, not trouble.

12. Free from the Love of Money

- A person who does not judge everything based on money.
- An individual who uses money but it is not the driving force in his life.
- Someone who is not addicted to making, spending or saving money at all times.

> 4 He must be one who manages his own household well, keeping his children under control with all dignity 5 (but if a man does not know how to manage his own household, how will he take care of the church of God?),
> - I Timothy 3:4:5

13. A Well Managed Home

- Keeping his children under control and respectful of his leadership in the home are priorities for an elder.
- He does this with dignity, meaning that he is serious about his family's conduct.
- The true test for a good church leader is not if he is rich or successful in business (there is no mention of this in the Bible). The true test is how he has led and managed his home.
- One who does a good job at home can be expected to do a good job with God's family which is the church.

> and not a new convert, so that he will not become conceited and fall into the condemnation incurred by the devil.
> - I Timothy 3:6

14. Not a New Convert

- A man with experience being a Christian since leaders are often attacked by Satan in many ways.
- Leadership in any position, especially the church, can go to one's head and because of this a leader who is proud becomes vulnerable to temptation. "Pride goes before destruction" Proverbs 16:18.
- Unfortunately, when a leader in the church falls he often brings many souls with him. The caution is that the inexperienced elder who falls because of pride will receive the same judgment as Satan who also fell because of pride.

15. Good Reputation Outside the Church

- The elder represents the church, so any accusation against him also falls on the church as well.
- If a leader is disgraced because of his reputation he can be used as a pawn in Satan's effort to discredit the church.
- There are other qualities mentioned in the letter to Titus but these are the ones Paul describes here.

This is not an exhaustive list (we could add honest, kind, loving, etc.) but a "snapshot" of the type of man who should fill the role of elder, pastor, etc. Note that these qualifications (except for that of being a man and married) are all qualities of character and thus subjective in nature. This often makes the selection of one man over another a challenge because the church has to make a value judgment in choosing the best man for the job.

For example, in deciding if a man is suitable for the eldership, the preacher or existing elders must ask themselves the following question: "Temperate but how temperate to qualify? Gentle, but how gentle to qualify to be an elder?" These are qualities and attitudes that all Christians should have and cultivate. So how do we distinguish between different Christian men in order to choose those who will lead? The answer, I believe, is that a potential leader has all of these qualities to the degree that they are visible to others. For example, in the case of a well-managed home. A potential leader has a home-life that others know and approve of. Hospitable? A potential leader is well known for his hospitality because many in the congregation have already experienced it.

In other words, a potential leader's qualifications are obvious, visible and growing. You do not have to wonder if he is gentle or not confrontational because you have seen these qualities in him already. They may continue to grow, but they are already there. He qualifies, therefore, because the characteristics described in the Bible for such men are already visible in him to a lessor or greater degree. This follows the biblical guidelines for choosing men who possess the basic qualifications of leaders but leaves room for natural spiritual growth which these brothers will experience because of the nature of their work as church leaders.

Appointment of Elders

How are elders chosen and appointed? The only example and teaching we have in the New Testament concerning this is the following passage:

> [21] After they had preached the gospel to that city and had made many disciples, they returned to Lystra and to Iconium and to Antioch, [22] strengthening the souls of the disciples, encouraging them to continue in the faith, and saying, "Through many tribulations we must enter the kingdom of God." [23] When they had appointed elders for them in every church, having prayed with fasting, they commended them to the Lord in whom they had believed.
> - Acts 14:21-23

Here, Paul appoints leaders through prayer and the laying on of hands. The fasting and prayer to seek the Lord's will in making the right selection, and the laying on of hands to publicly authorize these men in their new leadership roles.

> For this reason I left you in Crete, that you would set in order what remains and appoint elders in every city as I directed you,
> - Titus 1:5

According to Paul's instructions we see that the evangelist is to appoint them. The term "appoint" means to raise-up which would include the process of finding, training and then authorizing these men to serve in this position.

Elders are not self-appointed nor are they chosen by a popular vote. They are selected, trained and appointed by evangelists and elders together when the church is simply adding new elders and not appointing them for the first time as was the case for Titus. This is done in accordance to the teachings and qualifications found in the New Testament.

The beauty of the system is that in other passages the Bible says that elders appoint or commend evangelists into ministry (I Timothy 4:14). This creates an ongoing cycle of growth. Evangelists appoint elders - elders appoint evangelists - evangelists appoint elders, etc.

6.
ELDERS, DEACONS AND THE CHURCH
PART 1

I Timothy 3:8-13

In the previous chapter we looked at the role of leaders in the church. They were to be mature married men who were experienced Christians with virtuous characters focused on spiritual, not worldly things.

We examined the terms by which these men were called and what these words meant: bishop (authority), elder (maturity), pastor (ministry).

We also reviewed the work of these leaders:

- Guard the flock against false teaching and false teachers.
- Promote unity, peace and growth.
- Minister to those who were weak spiritually and physically (sick).

Finally, we touched on how these men were chosen for their leadership positions: they were trained and appointed by a missionary, evangelist or by other elders in churches where leaders were already in place.

In the present section we will review the responsibility the church has in response to its leaders and follow up by looking at another group of servants in the church referred to as "deacons."

Response of the Church to the Leaders

There are several passages that deal with the question of how to treat those who lead or minister in the church.

> [12] But we request of you, brethren, that you appreciate those who diligently labor among you, and have charge over you in the Lord and give you instruction, [13] and that you esteem them very highly in love because of their work. Live in peace with one another.
> - I Thessalonians 5:12-13

- To appreciate their work does not simply mean to be thankful. The point Paul is making is that the church should be aware of the work that elders perform on behalf of the congregation. The brethren should realize what, exactly, the elders are doing specifically for them. This knowledge will naturally lead to appreciation and a greater valuation of the elders' service. To esteem or consider them highly does not mean "in reverence" (bowing down, kissing the ring). It means that the congregation respects them for what they do, not just for the special role that God has given them.
- Note two things Paul mentions about the elders:
    - They oversee, have charge and are responsible in the Lord. God gives them real authority in the local church.
    - Paul refers to more than one elder since there is always a plurality of men in church leadership.

- How are esteem and respect in love demonstrated? The Apostle says that the congregation shows its esteem and respect by responding to the elders with kindness, cooperation and encouragement. Respect also includes the idea that we realize that these men are human, like us, and have a great task to do so we need to be careful not to criticize them unjustly since elders need God's grace and the church's patience at times.

Respect, therefore, is the first response of the church towards its leaders.

> Obey your leaders and submit to them, for they keep watch over your souls as those who will give an account. Let them do this with joy and not with grief, for this would be unprofitable for you.
> - Hebrews 13:17

The church must also submit to their teachings in Christ. As individuals with free will we still have the responsibility for knowing and following the truth. The main task of elders, therefore, is to maintain and teach the truth of the Scriptures to the church that submits to their teaching willingly and respectfully.

- If a church leader accurately teaches the Bible, we are bound to obey.
  - First, because it is God's truth we are hearing.
  - Second, because God's legitimate church leader is the one teaching or preaching this Word to us.

Of course, obedience and respect are given on the condition that they are leading according to the Spirit and the word of God because the Lord will hold them accountable for the church. The writer also adds a word of warning to the church not to make a leader's life difficult (by disobedience, laziness, indifference, rebellion, etc.) because those who do so will be punished.

Leaders have a responsibility to lead and the church has a responsibility to follow when that leadership is in Christ.

> Remember those who led you, who spoke the word of God to you; and considering the result of their conduct, imitate their faith.
> - Hebrews 13:7

A. Remember Them

- This is done when we pray for our leaders.
- We also remember them by implementing their teachings.
- Obedience, attention and submission are passive forms of respect.
- Prayer and implementation of their teachings in our lives are active forms of respect.

B. Imitate Them

- Look at their lives (their conduct) and see the fruit they have produced (the fruit of the Spirit: love, joy, peace, etc. - Galatians 5).
- Imitate what they have done in order to produce the same in your own life.
- Imitation is the system Christians use to learn and to grow.
    - We imitate God in Christ - Ephesians 5:1-2
    - We imitate the Apostles - I Corinthians 11:1
    - We imitate the elders/leaders in the church - Hebrews 13:7
    - We imitate other churches - I Thessalonians 2:13

- We learn and grow by observing and imitating the various examples that God has given us for this very purpose.

Elders are usually the first ones we observe in order to help us reach our full potential in Christ.

> [19] Do not receive an accusation against an elder except on the basis of two or three witnesses. [20] Those who continue in sin, rebuke in the presence of all, so that the rest also will be fearful of sinning. [21] I solemnly charge you in the presence of God and of Christ Jesus and of His chosen angels, to maintain these principles without bias, doing nothing in a spirit of partiality. [22] Do not lay hands upon anyone too hastily and thereby share responsibility for the sins of others; keep yourself free from sin.
> - I Timothy 5:19-22

Hold Them Accountable

Sometimes there are conflicts between leaders and members, or the leaders do not act appropriately. Paul touches on this in his letter to Timothy:

A. No gossiping. It is easy to get together and criticize our leaders, but this does not profit them or the church.

B. If there is a true problem, sin or offense, let at least two individuals approach the elder in question. It has to be a sin or an offense, not just something you do not like or disagree with.

C. Try to bring the matter to his attention. If there is no repentance, bring the matter before the church. This approach also serves as a warning to others that sin will be dealt with, no matter who in the church is guilty of it.

Do not favor one man over another. Treat all with respect and discipline all who sin.

D. Do not put a man in a leadership position too quickly. If he is not ready, he will fall and those who put him there will share in the responsibility for the errors that he makes because of inexperience.

Elders are ordinary men who are weak and sinful at times so there has to be a mechanism to correct or remove them if they are not fit to lead. Paul explains what that is in the brief passage we have just reviewed.

> [17] The elders who rule well are to be considered worthy of double honor, especially those who work hard at preaching and teaching. [18] For the Scripture says, "You shall not muzzle the ox while he is threshing," and "The laborer is worthy of his wages."
> - I Timothy 5:17-18

Honor Them

In the early church the **evangelists** went from place to place establishing churches or teaching and preaching at congregations that were already established.

The **elders, bishops, pastors** were the men who remained and led in the local churches. Paul encourages the church to highly value these men (double honor). Their hard work and great spiritual responsibilities were to be honored in the proper way just as an ox receives food for his work and a laborer receives his pay.

Leaders are worthy of double honor, the honor we give to all brothers and sisters in Christ as well as the additional honor due to those who lead well in the Lord's church.

Summary

Here are some of the common questions asked when teaching about church leaders: "How long can they serve as elders? Do they have to retire at a certain age? Should the church review their work and renew them every year?" The Bible gives no specific answers to these questions. It only provides us with the qualifications and work to be done as well as the proper response of the church to these men.

Based on the information we do have about elders, however, we can say that as long as a man remains qualified and continues to do the work properly, he can remain in leadership.

Word Study: Deacon/Deacons

> [8] Deacons likewise must be men of dignity, not double-tongued, or addicted to much wine or fond of sordid gain, [9] but holding to the mystery of the faith with a clear conscience. [10] These men must also first be tested; then let them serve as deacons if they are beyond reproach. [11] Women must likewise be dignified, not malicious gossips, but temperate, faithful in all things. [12] Deacons must be husbands of only one wife, and good managers of their children and their own households. [13] For those who have served well as deacons obtain for themselves a high standing and great confidence in the faith that is in Christ Jesus.
> - I Timothy 3:8-13

Another role that is described in the Bible is that of the deacon. Let's look at the word "deacon" and see what it reveals concerning those who serve the church in this capacity.

- Although the idea and example of serving is prevalent throughout the New Testament, the word "deacon" in reference to a person only appears five times, is used by Paul and mostly in one letter. There is one other instance (Acts 6) where there is reference to particular service that could be referred to as "deacon's" work, but the text does not use the pronoun for deacon in reference to the person carrying out the service. Instead, they are referred to using the word that described the service they were rendering (i.e. instead of saying that the waiters were serving tables, the text says that the men were "waitering").

Most words in the New Testament were in the Greek language of the time and eventually translated into other languages including English. Some words, however, were not translated but *transliterated,* meaning that a word was made up in the new language to represent the one in the original (Greek), usually a word that was spelled or sounded similar:

- The most common example of this was the Greek word *baptizo,* when translated this word meant to dip, plunge or to immerse in water. The word *baptizo*, however, was *transliterated* into the word *baptize*, a new word in English created to represent the word in Greek that was spelled and sounded similar (baptizo - baptize).
- In the same way, the Greek word *diakonos*, when translated meant servant or waiter in English. It, however, was *transliterated* into the word *deacon* in biblical texts (diakonos - deacon).

There is a reason, however, why this particular word was chosen to describe this person and his ministry. There were several words in the Greek that referred to those who served:

1. *Doulos*
    - Referred to a slave taken in war or purchased.
    - It was translated slave or bond-servant.
    - The word emphasized the idea of subordination and forced or obligatory service without personal freedom.
2. *Pais*
    - Youth or the children of slaves, or a youthful slave.
3. *Oiketes*
    - A household servant
      (today we would say a butler or a maid).
4. *Latrevo*
    - A hired servant or worker for hire.
5. *Hupereteo*
    - A manual laborer, tradesman, seaman.
6. *Leitourgos*
    - A public servant, priestly service, a minister.
7. *Diakonos*
    - Meant to wait upon (waiter), to be an attendant, to render service, to minister.

A brief look at the history of this particular word (*diakonos*) will help us understand why the Bible writers chose to use it more than any other (and there are more than just these seven) to describe the general service rendered in the church and the special servants called "deacons" in particular.

Words in any language go through changes in meaning and it is no different for the Greek language.

- The word *diakonos* originally referred to the meal attendant (hence the idea of waiter) in Greek society. In this context it was also used to describe the one who prepared the food for cultist or religious meals and feasts. In Jewish life, there was a strong emphasis on the importance of food (ceremonial offerings as well as food restrictions because of religious conviction). The Jews had a sense of benevolence and it was custom to collect and distribute food among the poor, even in pre-Christian times, as an act of service.

When Jesus came, however, He elevated what was common (servanthood) to a new level, making it a defining mark of discipleship and identification with Himself (contrary to social custom of that time that saw service as demeaning).

- Philippians 2:7 *...but emptied Himself, taking the form of a bond-servant, and being made in the likeness of men. - Doulos*
- Jesus injected the element of love into the act of service and re-cast what was a shameful thing in pagan society into a virtue for members of His church. In this sense we are all servants in the service of Christ.

In its initial stage, the first organized act of service in the church was the need to feed the Grecian widows in Jerusalem for which seven men were chosen. It is interesting to note that the words used in Acts 6 to describe the serving of these widows is the verb form of the word *diakonos*. The reason for this is that when it was food being served, distributed or managed, the word for serving or for the servant was *diakonos* or one of its forms.

The link, therefore, is here:

- When selecting a word that described the workers and the work done in loving service on behalf of the church by its members, the Apostles chose a word for "servant" that had always been connected with the personal, attentive and in some cases benevolent or loving service of food.

- With time the meaning of this word expanded to include two other things:
    - All service done by Christians was loving service, for food or for anything else.
    - Those special servants who by virtue of their special qualifications and the blessing of the elders, were appointed to a specific ministry in the church.
- With time, the word *diakonos*/deacon and all the words derived from this word referring to various kinds of service would be primarily used to describe church workers and church work (unlike the other words for service).
    - For service in the church, therefore, they did not use the usual words for servants common at that time *doulos/pais/oiketes/latrevo/hupereteo/leitourgos...* they used the word *diakonos*.

Like many other words that had multiple meanings (e.g. apostle/messenger - someone sent by an official [Barnabas - Acts 14:14] or THE Apostle or messenger - someone specifically sent by Christ [Peter, James, John, etc. - Matthew 10:2) the word *diakonos* or deacon, like the word Apostle, would have different meanings based on the context:

1. For example, any servant in the church rendering a service of some kind in Christ was a *diakonos*:

- Epaphras - *"just as you learned it from Epaphras, our beloved fellow bond-servant, who is a faithful servant of Christ on our behalf,"* (Colossians 1:7)
- Phoebe - *"I commend to you our sister Phoebe, who is a servant of the church which is at Cenchrea;"* (Romans 16:1)

2. The appointed servants who because of their qualifications, the ministry they fulfilled and the blessing of the elders, served as appointed servants in an office or ministry.

> Paul and Timothy, bond-servants of Christ Jesus, To all the saints in Christ Jesus who are in Philippi, including the overseers and deacons:
> - Philippians 1:1

- Bond-servants - *Doulos* = Apostles
- Saints - called out = all the saved
- Overseers - elders = appointed leaders
- Deacons - *diakonos* = appointed servants

The way to determine when the writers were describing a servant rendering a service or an appointed servant carrying out an office or a ministry was "CONTEXT."

> [11] And He gave some as apostles, and some as prophets, and some as evangelists, and some as pastors and teachers, [12] for the equipping of the saints for the work of service, to the building up of the body of Christ; [13] until we all attain to the unity of the faith, and of the knowledge of the Son of God, to a mature man, to the measure of the stature which belongs to the fullness of Christ.
> - Ephesians 4:11-13

Here, Paul describes specific roles for specific people in the church. These people received these "offices" or "ministries" based on the abilities given them by God, their spiritual qualifications and the blessing of the church leadership. We also note that each of these ministries was further explained in other parts of the New Testament.

However, each of these roles was defined in "context."

- All members of the church should prophesy (speak forth God's word) but only a few had, in those days, the ability and the anointing by the Spirit to prophecy concerning the future or speak directly from God.

- In today's church, all members are responsible to evangelize their homes and their community, but not all are called, qualified and sent by the elders as evangelists, preachers or missionaries.
- We should all provide leadership and be an example for our faith to the world but not every member is qualified and called to serve as an elder.
- Every member should learn and teach each other the word of God, but not all have the skill and the confirmation from the church leaders to teach classes on Bible subjects.

In the same way, we all serve the body as Christians in one way or another, but not all are qualified spiritually and technically to serve as appointed servants or deacons with a specific ministry or office. Paul does not describe this here in Ephesians 4 but he does so in I Timothy 3.

And so, the word deacon can mean any servant in the church, but most times it refers to those who have been selected by the church and appointed by the elders to carry out a specific ministry. Again, determining the exact meaning depends on the context of the passage where the words are located.

Summary

In the following chapter we will look at the qualifications of deacons and also address the issue of women serving as appointed deacons (deaconess) in the church. There are many opinions about this and we will see what Paul teaches Timothy on this matter.

One last question for this chapter: what is the essential difference between elders and deacons?

- Many of the qualifications are the same.
- Both serve the church.
- Both are men.

1. Authority - Elders are given authority to lead the congregation (to oversee) and deacons are not.

2. Ministry - Elders serve primarily by teaching and giving direction; deacons serve in carrying out tasks.

3. Appointed - Elders are appointed by evangelists; deacons are selected by the church and confirmed by the elders.

7.
ELDERS, DEACONS AND THE CHURCH
PART 2

I Timothy 3:8-13

In our last chapter we talked about the meaning of the word "deacon," how it relates to the work of the church and how this role is different from that of elder. We also reviewed the different words used to describe those who served as leaders in the church. Terms such as elder, bishop or pastor all referred to the same person with each word describing a facet of his character or responsibilities.

I also explained that the word deacon is a transliteration from the Greek word, *diakonos*, which refers to an attendant or a waiter. In the church, it referred to the men who were chosen to do certain tasks based on their qualifications, experience and approval of the congregation's leaders.

Deacons serve the church under the direction of the elders. They are different from elders in that their main tasks are service-related as opposed to teaching or direction of the assembly. They are selected by the church and are appointed, ordained or commended by the elders based on certain qualifications laid out in Acts 6:1-7; Philippians 1:1; and I Timothy 3:8-12.

In this chapter we're going to look more closely at these passages and see what they say about deacons.

The First Deacons

There are only three places in the New Testament where deacons are referred to and where we can find information about their qualifications.

> [1] Now at this time while the disciples were increasing in number, a complaint arose on the part of the Hellenistic Jews against the native Hebrews, because their widows were being overlooked in the daily serving of food. [2] So the twelve summoned the congregation of the disciples and said, "It is not desirable for us to neglect the word of God in order to serve tables. [3] Therefore, brethren, select from among you seven men of good reputation, full of the Spirit and of wisdom, whom we may put in charge of this task. [4] But we will devote ourselves to prayer and to the ministry of the word." [5] The statement found approval with the whole congregation; and they chose Stephen, a man full of faith and of the Holy Spirit, and Philip, Prochorus, Nicanor, Timon, Parmenas and Nicolas, a proselyte from Antioch. [6] And these they brought before the apostles; and after praying, they laid their hands on them.
> - Acts 6:1-6

Here the term deacon is not found, but the verb describing their work and from which their name would eventually come is used. The church at that time was growing quickly and along with this growth came the responsibility for benevolence, especially the feeding and care of widows. The Hellenistic widows were women who were not from Judea or had originally converted to Judaism before becoming Christians. It seems that they were being neglected in the daily distribution of food (the unspoken charge was that there may have been some discrimination going on because they were not native or cultural Jews) and so a complaint which threatened the unity of the church arose. The Apostles quickly settled the matter by calling for *diakonos* (serving or waitering to be done in order to care for these women's needs) which the Apostles explained was not their calling. Their ministry was to provide spiritual leadership through their teaching and prayers on behalf of the congregation, not the distribution of food to those in need.

Their response was to advise the church to select certain individuals who could carry out this ministry. The Apostles also established the basic qualifications that these individuals needed to have in order to serve in this capacity:

A. **They established a limited number**. The Apostles limited the number of individuals assigned to this task to seven. That they assigned this many people, however, suggests that the care of widows was quite an undertaking requiring many people to properly do the job.

B. **They were selected by the congregation from among the congregation.** Unlike elders who were selected by the evangelist or by other leaders, deacons are first selected by the congregation.

C. **They were to be men**, not women. Peter specified that these servants were to be males, even though there were surely women who qualified (full of the Spirit and of wisdom). The ministry to widows would have been a natural place for women to serve, but Peter specified that men were to be chosen.

D. **They were to have charge** or to be appointed over the task. The Apostles were involved in this work before but could no longer carry the burden of it so they gave the charge for this task to others. The mistake we make in the church today is that we give the work to the deacons but not the charge over the work. Once the guidelines were established, the work was in the hands of these men and not the Apostles.

E. **The task was singular**. These men were chosen for this task and not to be assistants to the Apostles (if this would have been the case, they would have had 12 deacons and not seven). Deacons were the servants of the church, not the Apostles, in carrying out this particular ministry. This is why they were chosen among the brethren and by the brethren because they were to be the servants of the brethren.

F. **They had specific qualifications.**

- Good reputation - speaks for itself.
- Full of the Spirit - all Christian men have the Holy Spirit, but some demonstrate more "fruit" of the Spirit as they are growing in Christ.
- Full of wisdom - as deacons they also needed particular wisdom or understanding in practical ways.
    - In the Old Testament, God filled men with wisdom as artisans, painters or builders in order to build the temple.
    - In the New Testament, He still gives men gifts and wisdom to carry out the work of the church in various areas (building, administration, service, giving, etc.).
- People who can take charge - if you are given charge, you have to be one who can take charge and get things done.

There were no further complaints about food, meaning that these seven were able to take care of this problem.

G. **They can be different kinds of men**. The list of deacons includes Stephen, a Jew; Nicolas, a Gentile convert to Judaism who then became a Christian.

H. **They were ordained, commended**. Some people incorrectly think that everybody is a deacon, or question what makes a deacon a special service or role. The fact that one is chosen by one's peers based on specific qualifications and then approved by a leadership is what makes a role or service separate and apart.

Deacons have a special and separate role from elders, preachers and saints, by virtue of their qualifications, selection and commendation.

The second passage that mentions deacons and the first that actually refers to them as such is:

> Paul and Timothy, bond-servants of Christ Jesus, To all the saints in Christ Jesus who are in Philippi, including the overseers and deacons...
> - Philippians 1:1

Here Paul greets the entire church as a whole (the saints) and then those who have a special role of responsibility and service within that body: the elders and the deacons.

Summary

There are not many references to deacons in the New Testament, but from the first two that we have looked at we can conclude several things about them:

1. **They are men** who are spiritually mature that use their particular talents in special service to the church aside from the ministry of the Word. The ministry or service of the Word is that of elders and preachers; the work of deacons permits elders and preachers to concentrate on their ministry. This does not mean that deacons cannot teach or preach (Stephen was very eloquent) but they are chosen as deacons for the other services they render.
2. **They are selected** by the congregation from the congregation for service to the congregation and commended or ordained by the leaders (the elders).

3. **Their leadership** or authority is connected to the accomplishing of their tasks. They have charge over their ministry once it is defined by the elders (i.e. in the case of these seven men, their charge was to organize and maintain the benevolent ministry of food distribution to the widows in the church).
4. **There are no deacons without specific tasks**. Since the word and the context refer to the one who does a specific job, when there is no job, there is no deacon. However, a deacon can be given charge over a small task and still be a deacon (for example, counting the collection, cleaning an area, etc.). What determines the office are the qualifications of the man, his choice by the congregation, confirmation by the elders and the fact that he has a specific job to do. A congregation can have 20 deacons so long as they qualify and have work to do.
5. **They constitute no authority** as individuals nor as a group within the church. They are neither a committee nor a lobby; they are servants with a specific task. We do not hear them speak in the New Testament when matters are discussed or decided (Acts 15:1-ff).

Let us examine a final passage of Scripture regarding deacons.

I Timothy 3:8-13

This passage gives us some insight as to the basic qualifications necessary to be considered for this role as well as their standing in the body and how they were chosen.

- **Vs. 1-7** - Paul has outlined the basic qualifications for elders in the Lord's church. He immediately follows with qualifications for deacons.

> [8] Deacons likewise must be men of dignity, not double-tongued, or addicted to much wine or fond of sordid gain,

Insofar as character is concerned, deacons are to resemble the elders ("likewise"). The term "must" means that there is no question about the need to be strict in requiring these qualifications for this role.

- Men of dignity or "grave" signifies a man who is respected, not flippant or coarse.
- Double-tongued refers to one who is a hypocrite, insincere, talking behind other people's back.
- Not given to much wine, sober, not a brawler. Moderation in the use of wine as it was consumed at that time:
    - Mixed water with wine.
    - Drank low alcohol content.
    - Moderate drinking would not produce drunkenness.
    - These were not moderate "social" drinkers. They drank wine as their primary drink and had to be careful not to let it lead to drunkenness.
- Fond of sordid gain. In the original context, this expression meant a person who earned a living in a sordid or unclean way: gambling, prostitution, stealing or cheating, any way which is shameful as a Christian, also people who liked this type of living (e.g. grifters).

> [9] but holding to the mystery of the faith with a clear conscience.

- The mystery of the faith is the gospel. The way people were to be saved was a mystery that no one knew until Christ came and revealed it (Romans 16:25-26).

- Men who are able to believe and practice their faith with a clear conscience (not undignified, hypocritical, drunken, impure or greedy). Some believe the mystery but do not act like they do. Deacons believe and their actions demonstrate this.

> [10] These men must also first be tested; then let them serve as deacons if they are beyond reproach.

- Deacons are to have proven that they are qualified before they are appointed. The church will choose a man they see doing the work and living a good Christian life long before he is appointed as a deacon. I Timothy 5:22 warns against being too quick in appointing elders or deacons less they fail and the negative effects of their failure be blamed on the evangelist or elders.
- When Paul says, "also," he is saying that this period of testing is also required for elders. Men who are not already providing leadership, service and living holy lives should not be appointed as elders or deacons.

> [11] Women must likewise be dignified, not malicious gossips, but temperate, faithful in all things.

- This verse has been used to suggest that women should also be appointed as deacons (deaconesses) in the church. The arguments for this are as follows:
    - The term woman can either mean "wives" as in wives of deacons or "women" as in deaconesses or servants of the church.
    - In Romans 16:1, Paul commends Phoebe, a servant, or *diakonos* of the church.
    - There are some early writings that suggest that women served in this capacity.

- The arguments against are as follows:
    - Paul does not use the term deaconess here, only a word that means wives or can be interpreted as women. Had he used the term deaconess, there would be no confusion.
    - The context of this passage is a list of qualifications for men as deacons and this reference to wives would seem natural as instruction to the wives of not only deacons but elders as well. The wives of these men would be involved with people and the work of their husbands and so their character and conduct had to be above reproach as well (he lists elders and deacons and then the women or wives of these men).

The only examples that we have of deacons doing their work shows that men were doing it. Acts 6:1-6 sees the Apostles specifying men to be selected. Here we have two opportunities by different Apostles to establish women in the role of deacon, but both times Peter and Paul specify men.

- What we do see in the New Testament, however, are women serving, *diakonosing* (waitering) in a variety of ways:
    - Women supporting Jesus' ministry - Luke 8:3
    - Women praying in the upper room - Acts 1
    - Dorcas making clothing for the poor - Acts 9
    - Mary the mother of Mark offering her home as a meeting place for the Apostles - Acts 12
    - Lydia offering hospitality to Paul - Acts 16
    - Priscilla offering her house to Paul and along with her husband, Aquila, having a Bible study with Apollos - Acts 18
    - Phoebe delivering a letter to Paul in Rome - Romans 16:1 (Here the Greek word *diakonos* is used in its "messenger" sense).

Women, therefore, are not among those chosen by the church and set before the leadership to be appointed as deacons. On the other hand, there are many men who serve in a variety of ways at different times also, but not all of them are set forth as deacons either.

The point here is this:

- All Christians, men and women, serve; they all waiter, take messages, work on behalf of the body.

- Only some of the men who are qualified are chosen by the church and appointed by the elders to be responsible for certain tasks, and these are referred to as deacons.

In the verse we are considering (vs. 11), I believe Paul refers to the wives of deacons and he says that as wives of deacons they also must:

- Be dignified (same as deacon).
- Not malicious gossips. It is never acceptable to be a gossip, but a deacon's wife must especially be careful in this regard since she, through her husband, is involved with many areas of the work and people in the church.
- Temperate - sober, sober-minded, not easily carried away by emotion, arguments or strife.
- Faithful as a general rule: in the faith especially, but also in service, marriage and friendship. She is a trustworthy person in general.

> [12] Deacons must be husbands of only one wife, and good managers of their children and their own households.

Paul lists the same qualifications previously mentioned for elders.

That no matter what his marital status - first and only marriage; widower; divorced; former polygamist. Now as a Christian he is a "one-woman" man. He is exclusively faithful to his wife. It is his "attitude" Paul is referring to. Other women feel comfortable and confident around him with never any question about his fidelity to his wife. Also, he must be a good manager of his home.

- If deacons cannot manage and care for their families (too busy, too lazy, too selfish or immature) how will they be able to manage the affairs and the work of the church?

A man's home and family says a lot about the man himself.

> [13] For those who have served well as deacons obtain for themselves a high standing and great confidence in the faith that is in Christ Jesus

Paul describes the reward for those who do a good job as church deacons.

- Increased measure and confidence in their faith concerning Christ Jesus.
  - Serving well re-affirms one's faith and strengthens a person's confidence in salvation, in God's care and in one's hope of heaven.

Have you ever noticed that the more you serve, the more you give and the more you sacrifice, the stronger your faith becomes? Stronger faith produces peace of mind, a joyful heart and a greater intimacy with God.

If this is the type of reward that comes with service to God, imagine the blessings on deacons and their wives who are officially appointed to service in the Lord's body?

This ends the section on special servants in the church. In the next section we will finish the chapter and see why Paul has written this letter in the first place.

8.
THE REASON FOR PAUL'S LETTER TO TIMOTHY

I Timothy 3:14-16

In chapter 1:3-4, Paul tells Timothy that the set purpose of his letter was to encourage the young evangelist to maintain sound doctrine and instruct others who were doing otherwise. Part of the work of a minister is to teach the Bible accurately while another part is to correct those who may be in error and consequently teaching what is incorrect. With this in mind, Paul writes to Timothy and includes the following information and teaching:

- Chapter 1:1-2 - Paul endorses Timothy and thus provides him with the authority he needs to carry out his ministry as an evangelist.
- Chapter 1:3-11 - The presence of false teachers and doctrines as well as the need for correction are noted.
- Chapter 1:12-17 - Paul's witness of his own conversion and appointment as an Apostle of Jesus.
- Chapter 2:1-7 - The need and subject of prayer is developed.
- Chapter 2:8 - Who and how prayer is to be offered.

- Chapter 2:9-15 - The role and position of men and women in the church in general.
- Chapter 3:1-7 - The duties and qualifications of elders are outlined.
- Chapter 3:8-13 - The duties and qualifications of deacons and the wives of elders and deacons are also provided.

These are the verses and subjects that we have covered so far in our study.

In the last section of chapter 3:14-16, Paul himself will summarize the instructions that he has thus far given to Timothy.

Mystery of Godliness — I Timothy 3:14-16

> I am writing these things to you, hoping to come to you before long;
> - I Timothy 3:14

We have a shift here as Paul describes some of his present circumstances and plans to see Timothy in person in order to provide more in-depth teaching.

> but in case I am delayed, I write so that you will know how one ought to conduct himself
> - I Timothy 3:15a

In case he is delayed, however, he includes the written instructions in this letter so Timothy can handle the situation himself. Paul repeats the idea that what he writes has a specific goal: to instruct the members of the church concerning their conduct. This is the main reason for his instructions on prayer, the role of men and women, and the selection process for elders and deacons. Paul says that as Christians we have a specific way to act, to organize ourselves and relate to each other as members of the church.

> in the household of God, which is the church of the living God, the pillar and support of the truth.
> - I Timothy 3:15b

Note how he refers to the church:

A. **Household of God** – God is the Father, we are His children. We are related because we have the same Father and we dwell in His household which is the church.

B. **Church of the Living God** – The Christian church belongs to and obeys the God who is real and alive. This as opposed to the churches, philosophies, religions and ideologies that follow gods that are dead (pagans), ideas that are of men, religions that honor false gods, human traditions and man-made deities.

C. **Pillar and Support of the Truth** – The idea is that the main role of God's household, the living God's church, is to be the depository and promoter of God's truth. The church preserves the truth, defends the truth and proclaims the truth. The "truth" that he talks about here is explained in greater detail in the next verse where he will refer to "truth" as "the mystery of godliness."

> By common confession,
> - I Timothy 3:16a

This is a way of saying "as the church is in the habit of saying or singing," or "as I often say." The idea is that Paul may be quoting a popular hymn or psalm that was said or sung by the early church which summarized the great truths contained in the gospel message.

> great is the mystery of godliness:
> - I Timothy 3:16b

At first he says "truth," now he refers to this "truth" that the church is to preserve and proclaim as "the mystery of godliness." Two ways of saying the same thing. The "gospel" is the truth, is the mystery!

- **Truth** - in that the gospel explains who the true God is, what man's true condition is, how God has saved man from condemnation, what happens after death and who God sent as the true Savior.
- **Mystery** - This truth about God, man's condition, salvation and the future was not known in its entirety until it was revealed by Jesus Christ.

> He who was revealed in the flesh, Was vindicated in the Spirit, Seen by angels, Proclaimed among the nations, Believed on in the world, Taken up in glory.
> - I Timothy 3:16c

Here Paul either recites the hymn or summarizes its content. Either way, he lists for Timothy the main points in the hymn, the major ideas and the teaching of the gospel itself. The "truth" or "mystery of godliness" he says, can be summarized in the following way:

1. Revealed in the Flesh

> In the beginning was the Word, and the Word was with God, and the Word was God.
> - John 1:1

> And the Word became flesh, and dwelt among us, and we saw His glory, glory as of the only begotten from the Father, full of grace and truth.
> - John 1:14

The Incarnation: the belief that God became man in the form of Jesus of Nazareth. This is the first and foremost teaching of the gospel and the statement all believers confess as they are baptized into Christ. Every major attack against Christianity from the first century until today, usually begins by denying this or trying to change this to something less or something different. The church is the defender and promoter of this truth.

2. Vindicated in the Spirit

> who was declared the Son of God with power by the resurrection from the dead, according to the Spirit of holiness, Jesus Christ our Lord,
> - Romans 1:4

The resurrection. The vindication (confirmation) that Jesus was the Son of God and was speaking truth was demonstrated by His resurrection. In Romans 8:11 Paul says that Jesus' resurrection was powered by the Holy Spirit. To all who doubt, disbelieve or deny that Jesus is God, the Holy Spirit responds with the resurrection of Jesus to prove (vindicate) that every claim He made about Himself or His mission was true.

3. Beheld by Angels

Not only was Jesus' resurrection witnessed by hundreds of people here on earth, it was also witnessed by those in the spiritual realm as well.

> 11 But Mary was standing outside the tomb weeping; and so, as she wept, she stooped and looked into

> the tomb; [12] and she saw two angels in white sitting, one at the head and one at the feet, where the body of Jesus had been lying.
> - John 20:11-12

This means that even Satan (created as an angelic being) is aware of Jesus' resurrection, as well as the angels in heaven. Both the physical and the spirit world have witnessed the resurrection of Christ.

4. Proclaimed Among the Nations

Beginning at Jerusalem and outward to all nations, the truth about Jesus has been and continues to be preached to all men (I Timothy 2:4-6). Jesus gave this instruction to His Apostles after His resurrection and, many years later, Paul says that this instruction was carried out fully.

> [18] And Jesus came up and spoke to them, saying, "All authority has been given to Me in heaven and on earth. [19] Go therefore and make disciples of all the nations, baptizing them in the name of the Father and the Son and the Holy Spirit, [20] teaching them to observe all that I commanded you; and lo, I am with you always, even to the end of the age."
> - Matthew 28:18-20

5. Believed on in the World

Beginning at Pentecost where three thousand were baptized, we see that the truth has continually gained believers.

> [40] And with many other words he solemnly testified and kept on exhorting them, saying, "Be saved from this perverse generation!" [41] So then, those who had received his word were baptized; and that day there

> were added about three thousand souls.
> - Acts 2:40-41

As long as the truth is preserved and proclaimed, it will bear fruit.

6. Taken up in Glory

The ascension of Jesus into heaven.

> And after He had said these things, He was lifted up while they were looking on, and a cloud received Him out of their sight.
> - Acts 1:9

After completing His preaching, death on the cross, resurrection and final instructions concerning the proclamation of the gospel, Jesus is visibly taken into heaven. An actual preview of what our own transformation will be like after we are resurrected from the dead.

And so Paul finishes summarizing the "truth" or the "mystery of godliness" that the church is to uphold and promote by listing the doctrinal "highlights" of the gospel contained in a hymn or poem commonly used in the church of that era.

Summary

In the first three chapters Paul outlines four basic teachings for Timothy to receive and pass on:

1. There is a specific order and organization that needs to be followed in the church.
2. Leaders in God's church need to be qualified before being appointed to leadership roles.

3. Members of the church need to conduct themselves according to God's will and not be conformed to the image of the world.
4. The role of the church and its main duty is to preserve the teachings of Christ and proclaim the gospel to the world.

Note that a majority of the problems in the "Christian" world are a direct result of violating these principles. For example:

1. Many have abandoned the organizational model of the church outlined in the Bible and have substituted their own model. **This has led to division.**
2. Religious leaders are chosen for education, length of service, popularity or reasons other than the list of qualifications given by Paul. We even have homosexuals serving as bishops in some groups! **These types of departures have multiplied religious error.**
3. Church members refuse to let go their worldly and sinful attitudes when they are converted, or return to them instead of maturing spiritually. **This contributes to the general weakening of the church.**
4. Churches focus on social programs, youth activities and building projects but neglect to prioritize the serious teaching of God's word and the proclamation of the gospel to the lost. They have worldly success as organizations but **become spiritually unfruitful.**

Paul was aware that not all of his instructions would be followed so in the next chapter he will provide a series of warnings as well as godly advice to Timothy on how to deal with adversity as a minister.

9.
THE MINISTER AND HIS MINISTRY

I Timothy 4:1-16

In the first three chapters of I Timothy, Paul has provided information and instruction dealing with the structure of leadership and the qualifications of those who will shepherd and serve the church.

He has also provided a summary of the basic doctrines of the Christian faith which the church should defend and promote:

- The deity and resurrection of Jesus.
- The content and preaching of the gospel message.

These are the teachings and ministry the church has been appointed to preserve and share with the world. This is the church's unique mission.

In chapter 4, Paul will explain why it is so important that the church be on guard for its mission, and remind Timothy about the nature of his ministry.

Apostasy Predicted and Identified – 4:1-6

In this chapter Paul warns the church that there will be apostasy and that they need to prepare and guard for it.

Apostasy: an abandonment of former loyalty; falling away from a position.

> [1] But the Spirit explicitly says that in later times some will fall away from the faith, paying attention to deceitful spirits and doctrines of demons, [2] by means of the hypocrisy of liars seared in their own conscience as with a branding iron,
> - I Timothy 4:1-2

First, Paul declares that the apostasy will be a sure thing. It will happen. This has been clearly revealed to him by the Holy Spirit. Here the Apostle is prophesying about a future event much as the prophets of old had warned Israel about future calamities and dangers.

The "later times" or "last times" is the Christian age, from Pentecost to the return of Christ. The falling away or apostasy will come at different times and in different ways during this period. Paul also defines the apostasy as the falling away from the "faith."

- When it is "the" faith, it refers to the teachings of Jesus rather than belief or trust.
- Some will leave the teachings of Jesus for other teachings.
- Apostasy also occurs when one abandons Christianity for something else.
- Another type of apostasy is when one changes the teachings of Christ or of the Apostles.

Falling away from the teaching causes one to fall away from the teacher.

> If you abide in my word, then you are truly disciples of mine.
> - John 8:31

Conversely, if you do not fall away then you are not in apostasy.

Paul goes on to note various causes of this apostasy:

A. Deceitful Spirits - I John 4:1-3

These are not ghosts, but false teachers in the church and what they teach. In John's epistle, the false teachers denied the incarnation claiming that Jesus was only a spirit, not really a man. Paul will explain later what some of the false ideas being promoted by the false teachers are that he is dealing with here. He refers to these as "doctrines of demons," meaning, teachings not coming from God but from Satan.

B. Men with Seared Consciences

Another way of referring to false teachers. Men who have no qualms about promoting what they know is false. They know they are lying but do not care because they are motivated not by the truth but by greed, by desire for power and attention. Their consciences are, Paul says, "seared" or "scarred/no effect."

> [29] I know that after my departure savage wolves will come in among you, not sparing the flock; [30] and from among your own selves men will arise, speaking perverse things, to draw away the disciples after them.
> - Acts 20:29-30

Some are mistaken or deluded and teach false things; others teach false things knowingly to promote an agenda. The results are the same however: people are moved to fall away from the truth, from the teachings of Christ.

> men who forbid marriage and advocate abstaining from foods which God has created to be gratefully shared in by those who believe and know the truth.
> - I Timothy 4:3

Paul gives a few details from the teaching of those who were causing the falling away of some during his time. From generation to generation the type of false doctrine changes but it always causes the same result: apostasy.

In this case, the false teaching promoted ascetic practices to become more "spiritual." (For example, no meat, no marriage and other restrictions that would somehow increase one's level of spirituality.)

The "doctrine" behind these practices was called *dualism*, a form of Gnostic teaching.

- Basically it taught that man had dual natures: spirit (from God) and flesh (or matter).
- Spirit was good, flesh was evil.
- The goal was to unite the human spirit with God's Spirit.
- There were two ways this could be done:
    - Very strict restrictions (certain foods, marriage) on the flesh (evil) so that the spirit could be released.

      - or -

    - Indulge the flesh completely since it is not connected to the spirit. When you die, the spirit will go to God anyways.

The debates and teachings argued for one or the other of these positions.

It seems that few were persuaded to accept the idea of complete liberation of the flesh since this was so against

Christian teaching and morality as well as Jewish teaching and custom. However, the idea of punishing the flesh and restricting one's body resonated with Christians who were trying to live pure and moral lives.

Gnostic teaching was wrong in many ways:

- Both the spirit and the flesh in man were given by God and created good (Genesis 1:31).
- Sin, which is disobedience of God's commands and will, is what is evil, not the flesh (I John 3:4).
- What a person does with his flesh (his body) affects his spirit (Romans 6:23).
- Restricting ourselves from food or lawful sexual activity does not increase our spirituality. Increasing our love for God by abstaining from sin and loving others, this increases our spirituality (John 13:35).

Paul emphasizes the fact that it was God Himself who provided all kinds of food, as well as the union of marriage in order to be blessings, not causes for sin.

Those who know the truth and believe it know these things and are able to eat and marry with a clear and grateful conscience.

> [4] For everything created by God is good, and nothing is to be rejected if it is received with gratitude; [5] for it is sanctified by means of the word of God and prayer.
> - I Timothy 4:4-5

Paul goes on to qualify a Christian's attitude and approach to not only food and marriage, but all things created by God. If God created it, it was essentially good.

- We know that some use good things for evil purposes but this is man's fault, not God's.
  - God created sex for marriage, not for pornography.
  - God created plants for medicine, not for drug abuse.

We can be assured and accept what God has given in good conscience for three reasons:

1. **He tells us** that what He wants in return for His blessings is gratitude, not denial of His blessings. He is more pleased if we say thank you for the food we eat than if we deny ourselves the food He gives us.

2. **We can know for sure** what is acceptable to Him or not from His Word.

- **Food**: Mark 7:18-23; Colossians 2:16. Food cannot make us more or less pleasing to God and those who say so are false teachers.
- **Marriage**: I Corinthians 9:3-5; I Timothy 3:2; Hebrews 13:4). If the Apostles were married, everyone could be married. The only restriction in marriage is fidelity to your partner.

- The reason people were led away on these issues was that they did not rely on God's word. If God permits and blesses (or sanctifies), then man can receive happily.

3. **Prayer purifies.** We live in a sinful world. We ourselves are sinners and imperfect (even though we are forgiven). What enables us to use and to eat the things of this world and to live with our spouses (even though we are both sinners) is the purifying power of prayer.

In the chain of people and events that bring me my food from the farm to my plate, who knows what injustices have been committed?

- Maybe the farmer is greedy or cruel.
- The processor of my food is an adulterer.
- The store where I bought it is robbing its employees.
- The person who wrapped my groceries is a blasphemer of God.
- And of course, I myself am a sinner needing grace and forgiveness each day.

If I knew all these things to be true, how could I eat this food with a clear conscience? Paul says that our prayers of thanksgiving and blessing before God sanctify and purify our hands and our food so we can eat it with grateful hearts and clear consciences. If it were not so, we would feel guilty every time we ate because we knew that so many in the world were starving and yet we had enough to eat.

False Teaching or Immaturity?

Before we go on to the next section in I Timothy, I want to say a word about extremes.

Many times we read this passage in I Timothy or the passage in Galatians 1:6-9 about false teachers and assume that we can accuse anyone who disagrees with us on doctrine of being a "false teacher." We need to understand that the apostasy is a reference to those who were falling away from the "gospel" and its message which Paul summarized in verse 16 of chapter 3.

- Jesus is the divine Son of God and He came in the flesh.
- He died on the cross and was resurrected.
- The gospel message is that we are saved by God's grace through faith in Jesus Christ expressed in repentance and baptism.

- He went back to heaven and will return again.

False teaching was any doctrine that attacked or tried to change or deny these basic tenets of the gospel message.

Someone who believes it is acceptable to worship with an instrument may be mistaken biblically or require more teaching to become more mature, but it would be an over-statement to call such a person a "false-teacher."

In the Bible this accusation was reserved for those who taught things that undermined the gospel itself which include the main points I have mentioned here.

In the Bible, people were disciplined or excommunicated for three things:

- False teaching of the gospel (Galatians 1:6-9).
- Divisiveness; causing trouble between members (Romans 16:17).
- Gross public immorality (unrepented public adultery, etc.) (I Corinthians 5:1).

But someone who disagrees or believes something different on issues that are not pertinent to one's salvation; or someone who is just difficult to get along with; or someone who has failed in marriage or is struggling with sexual sins - these are not causes to accuse people of false-teaching or to disfellowship them. These are matters of growth and spiritual maturity where we need to be patient with each other, open to listen and learn, able to put up with the weaknesses of others in order to maintain unity, and forgiving those who struggle with various sins knowing that we are not here to judge our brothers but to love and help them know and do what is right (Ephesians 4:11-13).

Our response to immaturity is maturity!

The Good Minister

After having dealt with the danger of apostasy, Paul gives four exhortations or encouragements to Timothy as a minister. They are just as true for ministers today as they were for Timothy two thousand years ago.

1. Point Out What is True From What is False

> In pointing out these things to the brethren, you will be a good servant of Christ Jesus, constantly nourished on the words of the faith and of the sound doctrine which you have been following.
> - I Timothy 4:6

Some Bibles say "putting into remembrance" but the meaning is the same.

Paul refers back to the teaching he has given in the previous verses and tells him to point these teachings out to the church: remind them often of these things. He not only has to remind the church, but he also must keep these things in mind and grow in his knowledge and assurance of these things (the divinity of Christ, His resurrection, the message of the gospel).

Today we would say, "the best defense is offense." Paul tells Timothy that the best way to protect himself and the church from false doctrine is to continually be absorbed in and teaching what is true.

2. Practice and Teach Personal Spiritual Discipline

> [7] But have nothing to do with worldly fables fit only for old women. On the other hand, discipline yourself for the purpose of godliness; [8] for bodily discipline is only of little profit, but godliness is profitable for all

> things, since it holds promise for the present life and also for the life to come. [9] It is a trustworthy statement deserving full acceptance. [10] For it is for this we labor and strive, because we have fixed our hope on the living God, who is the Savior of all men, especially of believers. [11] Prescribe and teach these things. [12] Let no one look down on your youthfulness, but rather in speech, conduct, love, faith and purity, show yourself an example of those who believe.
> - I Timothy 4:7-12

Timothy should avoid arguing and debating the useless doctrines of the false teachers (which he describes as "old wives' tales"). A more productive activity is to discipline or train himself for godliness.

- In other words, do those things, activities, disciplines, that will develop a godly character.
- Physical exercise is good, disciplining the body is good, but training the spirit is better because the body dies but the spirit lives on.
- Preparing for heaven is better than preparing for life here on earth.

This was another "saying" of Christians at that time (verse 8) and Paul says it is a good saying because it points to an important truth. Timothy should practice and teach about spiritual discipline because it is this that serves best the Christian's ultimate hope and goal: living with God in heaven. Like a good coach, Timothy should demonstrate the spiritual discipline that he wishes to impart to the church as he trains them in becoming like God and being with God in heaven.

Those who oppose him (perhaps the false teachers who may have accused him of being too young to be taken seriously in order to undermine his influence) will be stopped, not by arguments and debates over foolish questions, rather they and the entire congregation will be won over, influenced and positively impacted by the way he acts:

- The way he speaks (with wisdom and truth).
- The way he conducts himself (in maturity).
- The way he treats others (in love).
- The way he lives (faithfully and purely).

Ministers are like everyone else, people are impressed more by what they do than by what they say.

3. Preach the Word

> [13] Until I come, give attention to the public reading of Scripture, to exhortation and teaching. [14] Do not neglect the spiritual gift within you, which was bestowed on you through prophetic utterance with the laying on of hands by the presbytery.
> - I Timothy 4:13-14

For some reason or other, Timothy may have stopped or restricted his public preaching. Perhaps the pressure from the false teachers was making him doubt his ability and effectiveness. People who criticize or second-guess you may lead you to lose confidence in yourself and in your abilities.

In verse 14, Paul reminds him of the way he was called into ministry (prophetic utterance - Acts 16:2) and ordained into service by the church leadership (laying on of hands by the elders). He is, therefore, a legitimate minister and as a true minister, he must focus on his work:

A. **Reading the Word to the Church** – The Bible was not collected and distributed at this time, only the Old Testament and some letters of the Apostles. Reading these to the church was a main way of familiarizing themselves with God's word.

B. **Exhortation** – Encouragement to do or avoid doing certain things according to God's word. An appeal to act and think as God would have us do so. They needed encouragement to believe the truth and practice spiritual discipline.

C. **Teaching** – The plain teaching of the truths contained in the Word. Instruction on the true gospel and on the person of Christ. Teachings on church organization and leadership that Paul provided in the first three chapters.

There is a lot to learn about in the Christian faith and part of the preacher's job is to teach the church about the faith, the Lord and Christian living. Note that Paul says, "until I come." He plans to do some exhorting and teaching himself when he comes but tells Timothy not to abandon these things in the meantime.

4. Persevere in Ministry - verses 15-16

Preachers/ministers are ordinary men who have been called and trained to serve in God's church. Like ordinary people, they become tired and discouraged for a variety of reasons:

A. **Lack of Response or Success** – The church members who do not grow spiritually, who refuse to mature, or who fall away from Christ or are always at the same point. Ministry is like gardening , if you weed and feed and care for the garden but it does not produce fruit, you become discouraged.

B. **Lack of Encouragement** – Unlike business enterprises where you get raises, promotions and rewards in response to your efforts, ministers are rewarded when their members grow in Christ. Some become tired of serving without any feedback or reward from the congregation for their work.

C. **Criticism** – Timothy was beginning to feel the effects of opposition and criticism, he was not preaching or teaching like he should have been. He was "gun-shy," (nervous and apprehensive). A steady diet of criticism and complaining without any encouragement or reward often drives ministers to quit and do something else that is less stressful. Sensing that Timothy was feeling tired and discouraged, Paul gives him an "exhortation" to persevere in his ministry.

> Take pains with these things; be absorbed in them, so that your progress will be evident to all.
> - I Timothy 4:15

"Take pains" means to focus on or be absorbed by the things Paul has just spoken of: pointing out true and false doctrine, practicing spiritual discipline, preaching the Word.

The idea is that Timothy, although a young man, had been with Paul for a long time. He was not a novice. He was a true minister. As he focused on his ministry, the church would recognize his maturity and the fact that Paul's trust in him to lead the church was well founded. Those who thought he was "too young" would have a different opinion when they saw him absorbed in his ministry.

> Pay close attention to yourself and to your teaching; persevere in these things, for as you do this you will ensure salvation both for yourself and for those who hear you.
> - I Timothy 4:16

Pay attention to what you are doing and what is being taught, and what you have been taught (the true gospel, by a true Apostle, to a true minister).

If he perseveres (continues), he will insure (guarantee) that he will maintain his own salvation (by believing and teaching the true gospel and living by it) and do the same for those who listen to his teaching and follow his example.

Summary

In the end, Paul tells all ministers to preach the gospel to the lost so that they will be saved.

- They teach God's word to the church so that the saved will mature in Christ.
- They persevere in their ministry as an example so that all will remain faithful until the Lord comes for us either in death or glory.

In our next chapter, we will begin a long section containing specific teachings on various issues and questions that concerned the church at that time.

10.
THE CARE OF WIDOWS

I Timothy 5:1-16

In the first four chapters of this letter or book, Paul has focused on leadership issues. He has provided the objective of good leadership which, primarily, is to preserve sound doctrine. Paul has also given a profile of the type of men who should serve as elders, deacons and ministers along with several verses describing the ideal character of their wives.

In chapter five, the Apostle addresses various difficult situations that may have been present in the church at that time, and in so doing help today's church deal with similar problems.

Attitude of the Minister – 5:1-2

In the previous chapter, Paul has encouraged Timothy to not let anyone look down on his youth or be afraid to admonish and encourage the congregation. In verses one and two of this chapter, he tempers this instruction by reminding Timothy of the attitude he should have when encouraging others.

> Do not sharply rebuke an older man, but rather appeal to him as a father, to the younger men as brothers,
> - I Timothy 5:1

Younger men are not to be rough with the older men, but appeal to them as they would appeal to their fathers. One could "correct" an older man, but not as one would correct peers. Timothy is reminded that he must maintain respect, even when he has to admonish an older brother or sister in the Lord. Younger men, also, are not to be despised because they are younger, but treated as younger brothers.

> the older women as mothers, and the younger women as sisters, in all purity.
> - I Timothy 5:2

The same kind of balanced approach is to be used for older and younger women when it is necessary to admonish or encourage them as well. "In all purity" does not refer to sexual purity but to the way Timothy admonishes all groups of people, young or old, men or women. In other words, the admonishing itself must be pure, without anger, pride, violence or disrespect so that Timothy himself not become the object of criticism by the way that he admonishes others. This would undermine his ministry on behalf of those he has tried to correct.

Care for Widows by Family – verses 3-8

At that time there were no social programs to assist the elderly, sick, widows or orphans. Families took care of their own, or people became destitute and in some cases were enslaved. It was especially difficult for women who lost their husbands because opportunities for work or remarriage were limited. In the church, however, the care of widows was a ministry practiced from the very beginning (i.e. Acts 6 - deacons appointed to manage food distribution for widows at the church in Jerusalem). Paul gives instructions about this special area of the church's work.

> [3] Honor widows who are widows indeed; [4] but if any widow has children or grandchildren, they must first

> learn to practice piety in regard to their own family and to make some return to their parents; for this is acceptable in the sight of God.
> - I Timothy 5:3-4

"Honor" in the sense of respecting as genuine for the purpose of assisting those widows who are true widows: women who through the loss of their husbands have been left alone, in need and thus, vulnerable. The general rule is that her family (children and grandchildren) should care for her. Doing this is a form of spiritual exercise that is pleasing to God and a show of love and gratitude towards parents.

> [5] Now she who is a widow indeed and who has been left alone, has fixed her hope on God and continues in entreaties and prayers night and day. [6] But she who gives herself to wanton pleasure is dead even while she lives.
> - I Timothy 5:5-6

There were two kinds of widows and Paul clarifies which of these was deserving of such honor. The woman who called out to God for help and was faithful despite her desperate circumstances was to be favored over the one who used her freedom from marriage to abandon God and return to a worldly lifestyle.

Paul says that there was a responsibility for both the family and the church to help widows, but not all widows qualified for this assistance.

> [7] Prescribe these things as well, so that they may be above reproach. [8] But if anyone does not provide for his own, and especially for those of his household, he has denied the faith and is worse than an unbeliever.
> - I Timothy 5:7-8

Timothy is to teach these two principles concerning widows and their families:

- Widows need to remain faithful to God, conduct themselves in all purity and rely on the Lord for help.
- Families need to remember that to neglect to help their own parents and children deny the faith in doing so.

Being a widow does not excuse one from being faithful, and being a faithful Christian means you care for your family members who are in need.

Care for Widows by the Church – verses 9-16

This following section is difficult because we do not have a lot of background information to understand the context of Paul's instructions. It seems, however, that the church in Ephesus had some sort of benevolence program for widows and the Apostle is providing guidelines for its organization and function.

The problem occurs when we try to apply this passage to the modern church context where widows have access to government or company pensions, along with the assistance that the church can provide. It helps if we keep in mind the following ideas we have previously reviewed:

- Some things in the Bible are "eternal" in nature (e.g. resurrection, baptism, communion, role of men and women, etc.) and never change from generation to generation.
- There are also "cultural" things in the Bible which change from one period to the next because they are human customs (e.g. wearing of veils, foot washing, etc.) and not eternal in nature.

The system they used to care for widows in the church at that time was based on the society and culture that they lived in. We can, therefore, take the "principles" and "lessons" taught from their methods and adapt them to our twenty-first century context today. For example, we do not wash feet to show welcome, hospitality and respect for our guests. Instead, we take their coat, offer something to eat, greet them with a handshake or hug, meet them at the door and see them out when they depart.

And so, the same is true with the care of widows by the church. It is different today than in that period because our society is different. We can, however, apply the same principles. With this in mind, let's examine their "system" as it is described by Paul in this passage.

> [9] A widow is to be put on the list only if she is not less than sixty years old, having been the wife of one man, [10] having a reputation for good works; and if she has brought up children, if she has shown hospitality to strangers, if she has washed the saints' feet, if she has assisted those in distress, and if she has devoted herself to every good work.
> - I Timothy 5:9-10

Paul lays out the qualifications for a widow in the church to be put "on the list." We do not know what "the list" is exactly but many scholars believe that it was a benevolence list containing the names of widows that the church helped on a regular basis (like in Acts 6:1). Some say this is where the practice of having nuns began, but there is no support anywhere in Scripture for this idea.

In any event, there was a benevolence list and there was a question as to the women it should include. Paul clarifies this in his instructions to Timothy:

- She must be widowed and at least 60 years old.

- The wife of one man. This does not mean married only once. She could have been widowed twice or divorced and remarried with her second husband dead. The point is the same here as in the instructions for elders. She was a "one-man woman." In other words, she was a faithful wife.
- She had a reputation for doing good and serving others.
- She brought up her own children, not abandoning this task to others.
- She was hospitable, especially towards Christians.
- She was known to be benevolent towards others in distress.

In other words, not just a widow but a widow who has been faithful and productive as a Christian.

> [11] But refuse to put younger widows on the list, for when they feel sensual desires in disregard of Christ, they want to get married, [12] thus incurring condemnation, because they have set aside their previous pledge. [13] At the same time they also learn to be idle, as they go around from house to house; and not merely idle, but also gossips and busybodies, talking about things not proper to mention. [14] Therefore, I want younger widows to get married, bear children, keep house, and give the enemy no occasion for reproach; [15] for some have already turned aside to follow Satan.
> - I Timothy 5:11-15

In these verses, we may get some insight as to why Paul had to write about this subject in the first place. There may have been some women who claimed the church's benevolence whose only qualification was widowhood but who were not living the Christian life. Paul was clear about who should not be put on the list for regular assistance:

- Any widow under 60 years of age.
- Those who returned to worldly living and sexual immorality after losing their husbands.
    - The "pledge" in verse 12 was not a promise to avoid remarriage. It was the promise to be faithful to Christ. Some younger widows were falling away from their original commitment to Christ by marrying pagans and espousing their religion. In addition to this, some who did not remarry but lived from benevolence were wasting their time as busybodies and gossips.

Paul then summarizes his instructions by saying that he wanted young widows to remarry rather than be placed on the benevolence list. Young widows on this list were less motivated to marry, but rather wasted their time or were drawn to sexual sin or marriage to non-Christians. Paul advises them to remarry, raise families, care for their homes and remain faithful to the Lord. This type of life, he said, was noble and blessed by God.

> If any woman who is a believer has dependent widows, she must assist them and the church must not be burdened, so that it may assist those who are widows indeed.
> - I Timothy 5:16

Finally, Paul speaks to women who for some reason may themselves be responsible for widows. For example, a single woman caring for a mother or grandparent, or a widowed woman with older widows in her family dependent on her somehow, like Ruth and Naomi (Old Testament book of Ruth).

He repeats the same general principle: if the widow in question is a true widow in need (as described before), the younger widow needs to care for her and not put aside this responsibility because she herself may be widowed. The point is that some widows may have been fine financially and supported by other family members. Paul says that this woman cannot place one of her widowed parents in the care of the church using the excuse that she is a widow herself.

If able, we are to help our parents no matter what our status is in life. In this way the church can concentrate on those widows who truly need help and can only count on the church for assistance.

Modern Application

What principles does this passage teach us for our day in the care of widows?

1. We are first and foremost responsible to help our parents and families. The command to honor our mother and father as well as loving our neighbor are first seen in the way we care for our parents and family. If we neglect to do this, how can we say we love our neighbor that we do not even know?
2. The church is responsible to help those widows among its members who have no other source of assistance. Faithful Christian women who have served the Lord and continue to do so in old age should be able to receive help from the church when necessary. Thankfully, we live in a society that provides many resources for the elderly, but in the end we are responsible when these are not available.
3. Marriage, family and the home remain a woman's first priorities. Of course we have more opportunities for women to be educated and trained for careers in our society today, but marriage, family and home have never been replaced by career in God's eyes, only in the world. It is more challenging for women today because they must balance careers and family, but they find the right mix when marriage, family and home are a priority and not merely extra baggage in their pursuit of a career.

11. DISCIPLINING LEADERS

I Timothy 5:17-25

We are in a section of Paul's letter to Timothy where the Apostle is talking about various issues of concern to the church. In the previous chapter we reviewed the instructions Paul gave for the care of widows in the assembly. The brethren at Ephesus were not sure which ones should be helped and Paul provided some guidelines for the care of those Christian women who were truly in need and deserving of assistance.

In the next section, Paul will instruct Timothy concerning the way one should deal with leaders who cause trouble. There was unrest in the church where Timothy preached and apparently some of it was caused by those who were, or wanted to be, in leadership.

The potential for damage to the church is great when the division or the trouble is caused by those in leadership roles. Paul cautions Timothy about how to deal with this situation.

Concerning Elders

Verses 17-25 deal with three subjects:

1. Honoring Elders

> [17] The elders who rule well are to be considered worthy of double honor, especially those who work hard at preaching and teaching. [18] For the Scripture says, "You shall not muzzle the ox while he is threshing," and "The laborer is worthy of his wages."
> - I Timothy 5:17-18

Paul describes three areas of elders' work: **ruling** (leadership), **preaching** (proclaiming the Word) and **teaching** (instruction and application of the Word in Christian life). Leaders in the church are to be busy and absorbed in these duties. This is fairly straightforward, the problem lies in understanding the next verse.

Paul says that those who do these things well, and make a great effort at these things, are worthy of "double honor." There are several opinions as to what "double honor" refers to:

- Double pay
- Honor plus pay
- Twice the amount 60 year old widows received
- Two kinds of honor: one for age and one for the role of elder

There is nothing wrong with an elder who devotes himself completely to teaching and ministry receiving a salary from the church. I do not believe, however, that "double honor" means that he should receive double the salary of ministers or others. Paul says "double honor" in relationship to the service they give and then provides two examples to illustrate his point.

- The ox receives food from the grain it is threshing.
- The worker receives something back from his work: the pay agreed upon for his effort.

The elder receives something back from those he leads and teaches: honor for his role as elder in the church, extra honor (double) for his extra effort and ability in preaching and teaching. An example of this extra honor is seen in the next section where Paul will show Timothy the care taken in dealing with elders accused or guilty of sin.

2. Correcting Elders

> [19] Do not receive an accusation against an elder except on the basis of two or three witnesses. [20] Those who continue in sin, rebuke in the presence of all, so that the rest also will be fearful of sinning. [21] I solemnly charge you in the presence of God and of Christ Jesus and of His chosen angels, to maintain these principles without bias, doing nothing in a spirit of partiality.
> - I Timothy 5:19-21

Accusations against elders need to be brought up by a minimum of two witnesses, and having three would make a strong case. The idea is that no charge can be brought forward unless there are two or three witnesses that do so. This protects church leaders from baseless accusations, gossip and jealousy. If there are not at least two or three witnesses at hand to prove the accusation, it cannot even be made! We often see people's reputations ruined simply because they have been accused of something. Requiring two or more witnesses to even make an accusation protects church leaders from losing their good names without cause. On the other hand, if the witnesses have a case, then this protection cannot be given to the leader.

- Those elders guilty of continuing sin need to be rebuked by the evangelist before the other elders so that they will be warned not to behave in the same way.

- Elders guilty of serious sin (fornication, heresy, etc.) need to be removed.

These are difficult instructions and Timothy needs to make sure that he acts fairly in every situation.

- It is easy to confront a person that you may have issues with or struggle with over control or power.

- Timothy, however, must be committed to following these instructions with everyone and not show favoritism.

In the church, it is easy to ignore problems when friends are involved, but when it comes to discipline, Timothy (the minister or other elders) must judge and act with impartiality.

3. Selecting Elders

> Do not lay hands upon anyone too hastily and thereby share responsibility for the sins of others; keep yourself free from sin.
> - I Timothy 5:22

The "laying on" of hands was a gesture used at that time to signify various things:

A sign of blessing

> Then some children were brought to Him so that He might lay His hands on them and pray; and the disciples rebuked them.
> - Matthew 19:13

A sign of healing

> Then again He laid His hands on his eyes; and he looked intently and was restored, and began to see everything clearly.
> - Mark 8:25

A sign of empowerment

> Now when Simon saw that the Spirit was bestowed through the laying on of the apostles' hands, he offered them money,
> - Acts 8:18

A sign of commendation

> And these they brought before the apostles; and after praying, they laid their hands on them.
> - Acts 6:6

We still use the laying on of hands as a sign of blessing and commendation, but not one of healing or empowerment. God still heals (and hears our prayers for healing) but no longer grants humans the miraculous powers given to the Apostles and transferred to others by the laying on of their hands (Acts 8:18).

What Paul is talking about here is the laying on of hands to commend or "ordain" someone into the office of elder. He warns Timothy not to "ordain" or put men into leadership too quickly, meaning without making sure they qualify and are tested first. If he does, and because of this they stumble into error or sin, Timothy will share a portion of responsibility and guilt for their sins or failure.

Timothy is ultimately responsible for not getting involved in others' sins by ordaining them too quickly.

Concerning Timothy – 5:23-25

In the last section, Paul continues to talk about elders but does so in an indirect way.

> No longer drink water exclusively, but use a little wine for the sake of your stomach and your frequent ailments.
> - I Timothy 5:23

It seems that Timothy only drank water (which was contrary to the custom of the day). Perhaps he did this to make sure no one would accuse him of any type of abuse. But Timothy's habit made him vulnerable to illness (because the water in that day was often impure). If he fell ill, he wouldn't be able to carry out his work so Paul encourages him to drink wine in moderation in order to maintain good health. If he, as a leader, was sick from dysentery or other ailments, he would not be able to be an effective leader.

This is not a general command for all Christians to drink wine (since our water is treated and safe). But, on the other hand, it is a passage that makes it difficult to defend the idea that drinking wine is a sin. Keep in mind, however, that the wine of that day contained no more than three or four percent alcohol (today it has 12 to 13 percent) and the custom was to add water to the wine to further dilute the alcohol content (biblestudytools.com).

Timothy has an important role to play in appointing and training leaders in the church and he cannot do this if he is constantly ill.

This section is a summary statement regarding the entire issue of choosing or rejecting different men for the position of leadership in the church beginning in verse 22 where Paul instructs him to be careful in being too hasty in appointing men as elders.

> The sins of some men are quite evident, going before them to judgment; for others, their sins follow after.
> - I Timothy 5:24

Paul, therefore, is saying that in the matter of choosing the right man for the eldership, do not worry about choosing the wrong person. When deciding about a man's worthiness, you will be able to see fairly easily his faults and weaknesses (the sins of some men are quite evident; for example, someone's arrogance or foolishness).

For others, their sins follow, meaning that their sins are "not evident," they are behind them (out of view). However, in the same manner, these sins also become evident when Timothy examines these men in the light of the qualifications Paul has outlined previously.

> Likewise also, deeds that are good are quite evident, and those which are otherwise cannot be concealed.
> - I Timothy 5:25

Paul states the same idea again but uses "deeds" instead of "character" this time. Good deeds are evident. A man's good life will be easily discerned because his good works will be known. Conversely, an evil man will not be able to hide his evil deeds, they will eventually be found out. Paul, therefore, warns Timothy about not appointing men to leadership too quickly lest he share the responsibility for their sins and errors. He then comforts the young evangelist by telling him that it will be evident who the good and bad men are by the fruit of their characters and lives.

Lessons

1. Elders are Human

We all know this to be true but many times expect them to be above humanity.

- No mistakes
- No character weaknesses
- No limits on their willingness to serve or put up with laziness or other bad behavior by members

Most of the time they also have jobs and families to care for and have volunteered to minister to the church family as well.

Of course, we owe them honor, obedience and respect as the Bible says (Hebrews 13:7), but in addition to these I say that we also owe them the benefit of the doubt. Let us not assume, for example, that an honest mistake is really a purposeful slight, or that a lack of attention concerning a need or issue is a planned insult or a proof that the elder does not care. There may be a perfectly normal reason for his action or lack of action (e.g. sick wife is or overtime at work) and giving him the benefit of the doubt should be our first reaction.

Not jumping to negative conclusions or not having a hair-trigger in getting our feelings hurt will not only help the elder do his work, but it will also spare us a lot of unnecessary turmoil when it comes to our relationship with various leaders.

2. Elders Need Both Encouragement and Correction

The worst case scenario for an elder is when he will listen and accept encouragement but will refuse correction. Elders need both encouragement and correction because they are human.

A. **They need encouragement** in order to validate their work. Encouragement answers their main question, "Is what I am doing making a difference?" A positive word, a note of appreciation, a hug, all of these say to the elder that his efforts are recognized, needed and appreciated. It is this type of feedback that neutralizes unfair criticism and fuels the elder's desire to continue serving.

B. **They also need correction** in order to protect their leadership and the souls for which they are responsible. Paul gives careful instructions on how to go about doing this so that a simple course correction about an elder's attitude, behavior or teaching does not turn into a public spectacle disrupting the peace and unity of the church.

Correcting leaders can yield a tremendous amount of good for the elder (who through humility will grow spiritually) and the congregation (who will benefit from the renewed spirit of the corrected elder). Elders have a heavy load of responsibility given to them by God, but if they are encouraged often and receive correction in humility, both the man and the church will benefit.

12. PAUL'S TEACHING ON SLAVERY

I Timothy 6:1-2

We are in the last chapter of Paul's first letter to Timothy containing teaching and specific instructions covering a wide range of topics:

- Initial instruction to guard good doctrine and maintain his ministry
- Teaching on the roles of men and women in public worship assemblies
- Profiles of the type of men to serve as elders and deacons and the qualities that the wives of these men should possess
- Warning about apostasy
- Guidelines for a minister's work and conduct
- Instructions on how to conduct a benevolence program for widows in the church
- Teaching on the church's proper attitude towards elders and the manner of correcting them when necessary

The final chapter will continue to deal with various church issues that may have previously been raised by Timothy or that Paul was in some way aware of, having spent several years (54-57 AD) in that church himself.

Master and Slave Relationships

> [1] All who are under the yoke as slaves are to regard their own masters as worthy of all honor so that the name of God and our doctrine will not be spoken against. [2] Those who have believers as their masters must not be disrespectful to them because they are brethren, but must serve them all the more, because those who partake of the benefit are believers and beloved. Teach and preach these principles.
> - I Timothy 6:1-2

There are many who accuse Christianity of promoting slavery because, as we see here, Paul does not denounce the evil of slavery that existed at that time. How can we answer such accusations?

Let us review some information about slavery in the ancient world as well as how it was practiced in both Old and New Testament times among the Jews.

Slavery in Old Testament Period

In Old Testament times among pagan nations as well as among the Jews, there were many ways that a person became a slave:

1. The most common were those people enslaved as the result of war. The losers often ended up as slaves of the winners (Genesis 14:21).
2. Some were sold into slavery by their family or nation (Genesis 17:12).
3. Many were born into slavery (Genesis 15:3).

4. At times, a person became a slave in order to make restitution for a crime. There were no formal prisons so slavery was a form of punishment often used (Exodus 22:3).
5. Slavery was also the result when someone defaulted on debts (II Kings 4:1).
6. There was also self-sale into slavery in order to escape poverty and destitution (Exodus 21:2-6).
7. Kidnapping and piracy were criminal forms of slavery but not permitted among Jews (Exodus 21:16).

When discussing slavery in the Old Testament, therefore, one must differentiate between how it was practiced among pagans and Jews. Among pagans, like the Greeks or the Romans, slavery was commerce. Slaves in ancient times were not considered human, being property to be bought and sold.

Slavery existed among the Jews but was tempered and regulated by law. For example:

A. A Jew could not hold another Jew in permanent slavery because of debt or self-sale. A Jewish slave had to be released at the year of Jubilee and have his property restored to him. Every six years, there was what was called a sabbatical year (the seventh year) where the Jews gave their land rest, no farming was permitted (Leviticus 25:2).

After seven cycles of sabbatical years (7x7=49), on the 50th year, they celebrated what was called the year of Jubilee (from the Hebrew word "horn," referring to a ram's horn or trumpet). On this year, all debts were forgiven, Jewish slaves were freed and land that had been sold reverted back to the original owner. How close or how far the contract was made to the year of Jubilee determined the value of land and debts.

The point of this Law was to remind people that they did not own the land (nor the slaves), all belonged to God. It also guaranteed that the original borders for each tribe would remain the same and no tribe would increase by commercial trade over the other.

B. Among the Jews there were also other laws which protected female slaves and families from abuse. For example, if a female slave married her master or her master's son, she would be freed. If her master did not provide for her or divorced her, she would be freed (Exodus 21:7-11).

Even foreign slaves purchased or captured in war were included in the covenant through circumcision and participation in the festivals and feast days (Exodus 12:44).

C. Slavery did exist among the Jews of the Old Testament but it was not the basis of their economy or military. It was practiced in a more humane way among God's people where there were laws protecting the treatment of slaves (i.e. it was against the law to kill a slave, but legal in the pagan world).

We have to judge them in light of the degree of enlightenment that they had at that time. What they did (slavery) was morally wrong according to the knowledge and revelation we have today in the teachings of Christ, but for that period and according to their understanding, they were not sinning.

Slavery in the New Testament

By New Testament times, attitudes about slavery were changing drastically but there were still differences between Jewish and Gentile practices. Estimates of the total number of slaves in the Roman Empire show that as many as one third of the population were slaves.

We have to be careful, however, in the way we see the slavery of that time.

- Although morally wrong, the slavery of the Roman Empire was not the same as the slavery of the 18th-19th century slave trade that took place in the U.S.

- In the U.S., slavery was a strong economic factor for the Southern states at that time. Slaves were not considered fully human, and were bought and sold as property with no rights or chance for freedom.
- In the first century, there was relative peace and so there were few slaves from war or kidnapping.
- Most were domestic slaves or those who had become slaves through indebtedness.
- Slaves were not the basis of the economy but were contributors to it.
- At that time, owning slaves was a mark of prestige and wealth.
- Slaves learned trades (usually the same as their masters') and worked side by side with them sharing in the prosperity.
- There was a hierarchy of slaves according to experience, training, etc. and some were responsible for managing others, even running their own businesses under their master's patronage.

In the Roman Empire, there was a movement towards granting more slaves their freedom (called "manumission"). Paul the Apostle said he was born a "free man." This was a gift that Rome had bestowed on the province of Cilicia and the major city of Tarsus by Pompeii in 64 BC, probably for the cooperation of the people with the government.

Records of the time show that society was slowly recognizing that slavery was not a good economic and social model and this pushed a trend to allow freedom to more slaves. As a matter of fact, the Roman government had to put limits on how rapidly foreign slaves were freed into Roman society for fear of diluting the citizenry class of Rome.

Slavery in the First Century Church

None of the Apostles were slaves or had slaves.

The most common form of slavery in Judah at the time were "household" slaves. Note that Jesus acknowledges but does not condemn the existence of this system in many of His teachings and parables (Matthew 10:24; John 13:16).

It was a social reality in that time but did not cause social unrest. It was part of the system that no one questioned because the people did not have the "Western" mindset that we have inherited over two millennia of social change and progress.

Once the gospel was preached to the Gentiles, however, there were established, at first, mixed churches with Jews and Gentiles, and with time churches made up of both slave and free, even with masters and slaves within the same "household" congregations (e.g. the "jailer's" household, Lydia's household - in Acts).

The question often asked is, "Once the gospel was brought to the Jews and Gentiles, slave and free, why was slavery not expressly denounced by the Apostles?" Three reasons:

1. As a social system, slavery was already passing away

Paul teaches from a positive perspective, encouraging how slaves and masters should relate to one another to promote peace and harmony (I Corinthians 7:21-22; Ephesians 6:8; Colossians 3:22; 4:1).

The Apostles were sent to preach the gospel of salvation to all (slave and free), not to promote social reform for an evil system that was already in decline.

2. There was nothing to replace it

At the time, there was no great middle class to absorb newly freed slaves with jobs, money, land and opportunity. This system, although not morally ideal, did provide stability for the poor, as well as social peace.

In Philemon 16, Paul sends a runaway slave that he had converted back to his master and suggests, but does not demand, that he be set free. Without money or family he would have to enslave himself to someone else to survive. There was no unemployment insurance then and no job training or welfare. As a matter of fact, domestic slavery was a kind of welfare for that time.

3. Slavery was only temporary

Christians were changed by their conversion, not by their social status.

- Masters became slaves to God
- Slaves became free in Christ
- All were equal in Christ (Galatians 3:26-28)

Life on earth is temporary, so whatever position you hold on earth will end in death. According to I Corinthians 7:21-22, freedom in Christ does not change your social status. If you are able to change your status, go ahead, it is temporary anyways. What is important is your station or position with God. With conversion comes many new positions and titles:

- Disciple (Matthew 27:57)
- Priest (I Peter 2:9)
- Household of God (I Timothy 3:15)
- Saved (Mark 16:16)
- Son or daughter of God (Galatians 3:26-28)
- Beloved (I Thessalonians 1:4), etc.

The point is that as Christians we all take on a new identity and position before God in eternity, so whoever and whatever we are here (male, female, slave, free, rich, poor) has little bearing on the final outcome of who we are in Christ. These terms no longer define us, they only describe our earthly status for a time.

Paul and the other Apostles knew this and also understood that the social order of the day was passing away to be replaced by something else. They did not denounce it, they simply guided masters and slaves on how to live in peace and love with one another in the existing world they found themselves a part of.

The role of Apostles, preachers and the church is not to dismantle the existing world order, whatever it is.

- Totalitarianism
- Communism
- Capitalism
- Multiculturalism

Our task is to build the kingdom of God within whatever world order we find ourselves in. We witness to the existing world that there is an unseen world that exists and will one day overtake the present order, and everyone needs to enter into it in order to survive the change when it comes. In the end the heavens and the earth and all that is in them will be destroyed (II Peter 3:10).

The only thing to survive will be the kingdom, that is the church, where all are free, equal and will inherit eternal life in Christ.

13. PAUL'S FINAL INSTRUCTIONS TO THE CHURCH AND TIMOTHY

I Timothy 6:3-21

Here's a review of the material we looked at concerning slavery as it was practiced in the Old and New Testament times:

1. Slavery existed among both pagans and Jews in the Old Testament, as well as in the Roman Empire and among Christians in the New Testament period.

2. The main difference between pagans and believers in those times was that slaves among pagans were seen as property, but among believers were protected to a certain extent by religious law and Christian principles, and were included in the practice of the faith.

3. We shouldn't compare the practice of slavery in New Testament times (mostly domestics and laborers) to the slavery of 18th-19th century America (a strong factor of the economy).

4. Jesus and the Apostles commented on slavery but did not condemn it nor rebel against it because as a system it was passing away and there was nothing to replace it in the society of that time. The message of the gospel was primarily given to reconcile mankind to God through Christ, not to champion social causes. It eventually had a beneficial effect on society that led to the elimination of slavery, but this was a benefit of the gospel, not its initial purpose.

As Christianity grew and spread, its positive impact could be seen in the fading away of slavery, the elimination of polygamy and a greater respect for the poor, women, children, the weak, elderly and the sick.

The yeast of the Christian faith has been seen in positive social change over the decades. Moral evil of every kind is eventually reduced or eliminated because it is not compatible with the Christian faith and lifestyle. For example, I started to smoke cigarettes when I was 12 and continued until I was 30. I tried to quit many times, heard every argument against it but only when I became a Christian did I finally quit successfully because smoking was not compatible with my faith, my Christian goals and the Spirit of God within me.

Let us now go back over the relevant verses in chapter 6 and see what Paul actually says about slavery.

Instruction to Christian Slaves

> [1] All who are under the yoke as slaves are to regard their own masters as worthy of all honor so that the name of God and our doctrine will not be spoken against. [2] Those who have believers as their masters must not be disrespectful to them because they are brethren, but must serve them all the more, because those who partake of the benefit are believers and

> beloved. Teach and preach these principles.
> - I Timothy 6:1-2

Note that Paul gives no instruction to masters here, only to slaves. He does, however, provide instructions for masters in two other epistles (Ephesians 6:9; Colossians 4:1).

He says two things to Christians at Ephesus who are slaves:

1. Honor or respect their pagan masters as a witness of their faith. Slaves could not preach or teach their masters, so the way that they behaved and demonstrated their respect towards their masters would serve as their witness (or condemnation) of their faith.
2. Do not take advantage of the fact that your master was a fellow believer (to disrespect or give less service because he was your equal in Christ). As Christians in different positions, both master and slave were interested in doing good to one another: the slave was to render good service and the master was to be fair and generous to his slave. Both people shared in the benefits that came from being Christians (the slave was able to give good service with a clear conscience and the master was free to provide fair treatment in a spirit of generosity without hesitation to his slave).

These principles about the master/slave relationship needed to be the basis for teaching on this subject in all churches where Timothy taught or where this subject was taught.

General Instructions — 6:3-21

In this last section, Paul will give general instructions for those who minister in the church, and specific instructions to Timothy himself for his ministry.

1. Warning to Those who Cause Division

> [3] If anyone advocates a different doctrine and does not agree with sound words, those of our Lord Jesus Christ, and with the doctrine conforming to godliness, [4] he is conceited and understands nothing; but he has a morbid interest in controversial questions and disputes about words, out of which arise envy, strife, abusive language, evil suspicions, [5] and constant friction between men of depraved mind and deprived of the truth, who suppose that godliness is a means of gain.
> - I Timothy 6:3-5

Paul returns to one of his original points in chapter 1 concerning false teachers who cause trouble in the church. It seems that some were profiting financially from their false teaching and Paul suggests that this may be the true motive behind their efforts. He describes their method of operation:

1. They oppose the teaching established by Jesus and the Apostles and promoted by Timothy concerning the way to godliness (being like God, Christ, righteous, etc.).
2. They substitute the teachings of Christ with debates over words, obscure doctrines, controversial issues which give rise to arguments, division, evil thoughts and suspicion about others.

Paul also reveals the true nature and goal of these troublemakers:

- They pose as teachers but know nothing.
- They pretend to know more than the true teachers by their empty knowledge and conceit.
- Their minds are corrupted and this corruption is proven by what they produce.

It is not that godliness is a way to make money, it is that the true motivation for these teachers is the desire to make money from their teachings (which are false) about spiritual things (i.e. godliness).

Paul also mentions the idea of money as a way to lead into his next point.

2. Warning to Those Whose Desire is Money

> [6] But godliness actually is a means of great gain when accompanied by contentment. [7] For we have brought nothing into the world, so we cannot take anything out of it either. [8] If we have food and covering, with these we shall be content. [9] But those who want to get rich fall into temptation and a snare and many foolish and harmful desires which plunge men into ruin and destruction. [10] For the love of money is a root of all sorts of evil, and some by longing for it have wandered away from the faith and pierced themselves with many griefs.
> - I Timothy 6:6-10

He picks up the idea of godliness and gain (wealth) and says that, unlike the perverted teachings of the troublemakers, there is a relationship between the two: true godliness when accompanied by contentment is a great way to gain or prosper. The idea is that when someone is right with God (godly), he can be content with the basics (food and covering). Conversely, if you are not right with God, it does not matter what you have, you are not content.

The message, between the lines, is that it is godliness that creates contentment in the heart, not wealth. We have nothing when we are born and we bring nothing with us when we die, and whatever we accumulate in between does not have the power to give us the kind of peace and contentment provided by godliness!

Paul finishes with a warning against the love or desire for money. It is the root or the basis for many other evils in life. This desire drives us to say and do many foolish, dangerous and sinful things. The worst of these, of course, is that the pursuit of money draws us away from the pursuit of holiness, godliness and love, and replaces these with the pursuit of personal wealth and security, of power over others, and the accumulation of things and earthly pleasure.

The end result, of course, is that we exchange our souls for the things of this world.

> [17] Instruct those who are rich in this present world not to be conceited or to fix their hope on the uncertainty of riches, but on God, who richly supplies us with all things to enjoy. [18] Instruct them to do good, to be rich in good works, to be generous and ready to share, [19] storing up for themselves the treasure of a good foundation for the future, so that they may take hold of that which is life indeed.
> - I Timothy 6:17-19

We skip to this part because it is the natural point that follows the warning against the overwhelming love of money.

Usually the poor think, dream and pursue wealth to their own destruction. At times, however, gaining or having wealth is not a sin in itself, it is simply a challenge to one's spirituality if abused.

Paul, therefore, has a series of exhortations for those who already have wealth so that their wealth not become a cause for sin.

1. Make sure your faith is in God, not in the wealth you have.

2. Do not let your wealth make you conceited (thinking, "I am better because I am rich, I do not need anyone").

3. Realize that God is the One who provides wealth, not yourself, so be thankful.

4. Remember that wealth is uncertain but God is always there.

5. Use your wealth in God's service, not in your own, so that you become wealthy before God.

6. Pursue true life which is spiritual rather than the life that money buys.

In the end, rich and poor alike will receive what they have yearned for: wealth and pleasure on earth or eternal life with God in heaven.

3. Warning to Ministers - 6:11, 20-21

The final word in the letter goes to Timothy and to those like him whose task is to minister to the church.

> [11] But flee from these things, you man of God, and pursue righteousness, godliness, faith, love, perseverance and gentleness. [12] Fight the good fight of faith; take hold of the eternal life to which you were called, and you made the good confession in the presence of many witnesses. [13] I charge you in the presence of God, who gives life to all things, and of Christ Jesus, who testified the good confession before Pontius Pilate, [14] that you keep the commandment without stain or reproach until the appearing of our Lord Jesus Christ, [15] which He will bring about at the proper time—
> - I Timothy 6:11-15

His warnings and encouragements are based on the previous things that he has written:

A. Avoid the division and strife of the false teachers and the pursuit of wealth for its own sake. Run away from these things.

B. Focus your energies on spiritual goals like:

- Righteousness - right living
- Godliness - godly character and spirit
- Faith - being faithful to God and to the church
- Love - of God and of others
- Perseverance - abiding under the load and challenge of ministry
- Gentleness - meekness, the opposite of self-interest or self-promotion

C. Fight your own battle of faith.

He is a minister but he is also an individual Christian who needs to remain faithful until the end in order to be with Christ in eternity. In the end, all of us must fight the good fight of faith; it is not any easier or different for ministers. Like everyone else, Timothy confessed Christ in becoming a Christian and he must now complete the race set for him when he began the Christian life.

D. Preach the Word faithfully.

Jesus made the "good confession," that He was the Son of God, even when it caused His death. Timothy, as a preacher, must maintain this basic doctrine of the faith despite all obstacles. The job of preachers is not only to proclaim the gospel (whose central teaching is the divinity of Christ), they must also preserve the integrity of the message without changing, adding or deleting any part of it until they pass it on to the next generation or until Jesus returns.

> [20] O Timothy, guard what has been entrusted to you, avoiding worldly and empty chatter and the opposing arguments of what is falsely called "knowledge"— [21] which some have professed and thus gone astray from the faith. Grace be with you.
> - I Timothy 6:20-21

The balance of his exhortation to Timothy comes at the end of the letter.

E. Guard your gifts

Timothy has two gifts: one is the knowledge of the gospel itself received from Paul, and the other is the ministry of preaching received from God through the laying on of hands by the elders (I Timothy 4:14). These two gifts are both sides of the same coin that Timothy is to guard by not being drawn into the divisions and debates going on.

Also, he is not to trade the gospel for the false knowledge or philosophy that was being promoted at that time. He was a young man and could be seduced into joining the older and perhaps "educated" teachers who were promoting a false teaching with fancy words and personal claims to superior knowledge. Others had been seduced and led away but Timothy had to guard against this and remain faithful to his calling as well as to the message of the gospel.

Paul then ends the letter with the blessing "grace be with you." The Apostle includes all the blessings of God summarized in a single word: grace.

Doxology — 6:15b-16

> [15b] He who is the blessed and only Sovereign, the King of kings and Lord of lords, [16] who alone possesses immortality and dwells in unapproachable

> light, whom no man has seen or can see. To Him be honor and eternal dominion! Amen.
> - I Timothy 6:15b-16

These verses do not match the message Paul is giving to Timothy as far as warnings and personal encouragements. They are neither. They are a doxology or "spontaneous praise."

Paul becomes caught up in what he is saying to Timothy in this letter and simply breaks out into praise before continuing on with the subject at hand. As he talks about the eventual coming of Jesus, he is carried away and says: God, who is the most blessed of all sovereigns; the King of all the kings; Lord of all the lords; who is eternal; is the source of Light; is unapproachable by sinful man...

He and only **He** is worthy of honor and worthy to rule over all things. It is this God who will reveal the Christ at the end of the world, a time that only He knows. So Paul praises Christ, His message and also praises and worships the Father.

The doxology correctly praises the Godhead:

- The Father who sent Jesus to the cross and will reveal Him in the end.
- The Son who dies for sin and whose resurrection precedes our own.
- The Holy Spirit whose word Timothy must guard and proclaim until Christ returns.

This ends Paul's comments and our study of the first epistle to Timothy. God bless you.

II TIMOTHY

Although this is a second letter sent by Paul to the young evangelist, Timothy, the tone and circumstances of this communication could not be more different. Commonly regarded as Paul's last epistle, Paul's final letter summarizes his most important teachings and bids a touching farewell to a trusted and loved disciple.

14. INTRODUCTION TO II TIMOTHY

II Timothy 1:1-5

I have already provided introductory information on Paul the Apostle and Timothy the young evangelist in the first chapter of this book. In that section I reviewed the time and circumstances of Paul's first letter to Timothy as well as the relationship and special bond between these two servants of God (they were like father and son). The nature of their relationship, however, really shines through in this second letter.

In Paul's first letter he advised Timothy on the topics of church organization, leadership roles and how to deal with teachers who were attempting to replace the gospel with a new teaching derived from a mix of ideas taken from mystery religions, Greek philosophies, Jewish law as well as Christianity to produce a "Gnostic (knowledge) gospel." In reality this super-gospel threatened the faith and stability of the church, not to mention Paul's credibility as an Apostle and Timothy's position as a teacher sent by Paul.

This second letter is more personal in nature as Paul focuses on Timothy's state of mind while he battles the issues and people described in the first letter. It also provides a window into Paul's own personal struggles and needs as he faces the greatest crisis in his long and fruitful service on behalf of the gospel and care for the young church of the first century.

Background for II Timothy

A. Date

The letter was written shortly before Paul was executed in Rome by the emperor Nero, somewhere between 64-67 AD.

B. Paul's circumstances

After being released from his first imprisonment, Paul likely travelled to Nicopolis located in western Greece and planned to stay there for a while (Titus 3:12). When the persecution of the church by Nero began, he left there and travelled to the safer confines of Troas. It seems that he was forced to flee from that city as well since, in the rush, he left behind his cloak, books and parchments (probably Old Testament scriptures, II Timothy 4:13).

It was around this time that he was arrested on a second occasion and taken back to Rome for trial and execution. It seems that Alexander, a coppersmith, may have had a hand in his arrest (II Timothy 4:14). He was apprehended shortly after the burning of Rome by Nero, who blamed this destruction on the Christians in that city who were disliked by the general population. As one of the most prominent Christian leaders, Paul was an easy target for arrest.

C. Paul's second imprisonment

Paul's first imprisonment was caused by false accusations from Jewish leaders. This time it was the Romans who brought false charges against him (II Timothy 2:9). In his previous imprisonment he was under house arrest, this time he is placed in a dungeon. Before, he preached and taught freely all those who came to visit and stay with him. Now visits are restricted (II Timothy 1:17) and no one stood with him at trial.

ITALY
GALATIA
TROAS
CILICI
NICOPOLIS
EPHESUS
CORINTH
MALTA
CYPRUS
CRETE
MEDITERRANEAN SEA
JERUSALEM
DEAD SEA
EGYPT

He confidently expected to be released from his first imprisonment but has no such hope this time (II Timothy 4:6). The expectation of execution gives both urgency to his words of encouragement to Timothy and sadness as he bids farewell to a beloved brother and co-worker in the Lord.

D. The purpose of the letter

1. To encourage Timothy to be faithful in his preaching and teaching even while facing death, and that the preaching and purity of the gospel continue even in the face of adversity.

2. To set forth Paul's final testimony for his own faith before he died.

3. To ask Timothy to come and be at his side during his final days and bring along his personal effects (robe, book, parchments) when he comes.

This is Paul's last surviving letter. It has been styled as his last will and testament.

E. Interesting facts about II Timothy

- It is a very personal letter in that it refers to 23 individuals in four short chapters.
- Only Paul's letter to Philemon is more personal.
- This is the only place in the Bible where the names of Pharaoh's magicians, who opposed Moses and Aaron (Exodus 7:11), are mentioned: Jannes and Jambres (II Timothy 3:8).
- Paul refers to Timothy as a "man of God" (II Timothy 3:17), which was a title given to the great prophets of Israel (Moses in Deuteronomy 33:1, Samuel in I Samuel 9:6, David in Nehemiah 12:24).

- In speaking of his impending execution, Paul uses the term "already being offered" which in the Greek language meant that a sacrificed animal's blood was "poured out as a drink or liquid offering" on a sacrificial altar.
- Paul was executed by beheading. As a Roman citizen he would not (as Jesus and Peter) be subject to execution by crucifixion.

Based on the request made of him in this letter we can surmise that Timothy followed Paul's instructions in collecting his things, travelled to Rome to be with him at the end of his life and witnessed his martyrdom.

Outline

There is no main "theme" for II Timothy as Paul touches on many topics. He is wrapping things up and consequently giving final advice and warnings about several things. Here's a breakdown for a possible outline:

1. Greetings and thanksgivings
   - 1:1-5
2. Encouragement and instructions
   for evangelistic service
   - 1:6-2:26
3. Warnings and assurances for the future
   - 3:1-17
4. Paul's final exhortation, testimony and benedictions
   - 4:1-22

We will be following this general outline in our study of II Timothy.

Greetings and Thanksgiving — 1:1-5

Greetings - 1:1

> Paul, an apostle of Christ Jesus by the will of God, according to the promise of life in Christ Jesus,
> - II Timothy 1:1

Paul summarizes his life, ministry and future hope all in one verse.

A. Who he is. He makes no reference to his past as a Jew, Pharisee and persecutor of the church because all of that was dead and buried in the waters of baptism where he, like all other believers, came out of the water as a new creature in Christ: a Christian. And as Paul said himself (II Corinthians 5:17) *"if anyone is in Christ, he is a new creature; the old things passed away; behold, new things have come."* For Paul, the only identity he now acknowledged aside from that of Christian was as an Apostle of Christ, chosen and called by God. This role and identity not only defined his life and ministry but was also the major cause of his persecution by the Jews, torture and threats of death by the Gentiles and finally his arrest and looming execution by the Romans. And yet, despite all of this, in his last letter he continues to boldly identify with the One who is the cause of his impending execution. His entire existence is connected to Christ whether it is related to ministry or personal suffering or death - he only identifies with Jesus.

B. Paul's other reference (aside from who he is now) is what he hopes for in the future. His death is imminent and he acknowledges this by commenting on what will happen after his death. He joins the two ideas in this verse together by saying that his calling to apostleship sent him out to declare the promise of God in Christ - which he refers to here as "...the promise of life in Christ Jesus." The "life" promised was not just a lifestyle but a spiritual and thus eternal life for those in Christ or those who believe in Jesus.

So Paul begins his final letter, addressed to Timothy, by once again stating his faithful allegiance to Christ (apostle), purpose of his calling (gospel) and hope for the future (eternal life).

Greetings - 1:2

> To Timothy, my beloved son; Grace, mercy and peace from God the Father and Christ Jesus our Lord.
> - II Timothy 1:2

Paul uses a similar greeting in this second letter that he used in his first letter to Timothy.

A. The blessing - Grace, mercy and peace

1. **Grace** is the character and motivation that moved God to offer sinful man forgiveness and salvation based on faith in Jesus Christ rather than perfect obedience to the Law. That Jesus obeys the Law perfectly and offers His perfect life on the cross as a restitution or payment for our sins; that we receive perfect righteousness as a gift based on our faith in Jesus (expressed in repentance and baptism); this demonstrates how gracious God is.

2. **Mercy** speaks to God's ongoing love for mankind and His blessings upon both believers and unbelievers. He blesses unbelievers with life and everything necessary to make life worth living such as family, comfort, physical and emotional blessings, beauty and abundance, etc. He also continues to reach out to unbelievers with the gospel of salvation throughout their lives so that they might believe. In addition to this, He also blesses believers with all the same things that unbelievers have (*"..the rain falls on the just and the unjust.."* Matthew 5:45). And, of course, in addition to these blessings the Lord also continues to forgive and restore

believers who sin and fall short throughout their lives. This is something that is not available to those who do not believe (I John 1:7-9).

3. **Peace** is the result of God's grace and mercy towards the believer. A believer is at peace with God because his sins are forgiven and he no longer faces condemnation at judgment (Romans 8:1). A believer is at peace with himself because he can forgive himself for not being perfect. If God forgives you your sins and imperfections, you can forgive yourself as well. You can honestly do your best to serve God and live righteously without feeling stressed or guilty because both you and God know you are not perfect and have allowed Jesus to deal with that imperfection at the cross. When Satan accuses me in my conscience of not being perfect, I point him and my conscience to the cross.

A believer is at peace with others because his relationship with others is now placed on the higher, spiritual level. I no longer compete with or judge others because my task as a believer is to love others as Christ has loved me. This clear mandate for my expected behavior uncomplicates my life and brings an element of peace to all of my relationships.

B. The source of the blessings (grace, mercy, peace)

As in I Timothy, Paul repeats that the source of these blessings is God the Father and Jesus the Lord. What is notable here is that Paul places God the Father and Jesus on the same level and in doing so declares once again the divinity of Jesus.

The third similarity...

C. The recipient of the letter

This is where the two passages differ. Both letters are addressed to Timothy, but in the first letter Paul calls him a true child, referring to Paul's influence in converting him and helping him develop into spiritual maturity; in the second letter

Paul calls him a "beloved son" which is a more personal and emotional term.

Paul is confined to a Roman dungeon awaiting execution when he writes a final letter to this his closest associate and disciple, Timothy. In the letter he greets the young preacher with a familiar blessing that encapsulates what they both believe concerning the gospel, and he addresses Timothy as a loving son, made more precious to him in his last days. The contemplation of this loving and spiritually fruitful relationship moves the Apostle to give thanks in prayer.

Thanksgiving - 1:3-5

> [3] I thank God, whom I serve with a clear conscience the way my forefathers did, as I constantly remember you in my prayers night and day. [4] longing to see you, even as I recall your tears, so that I may be filled with joy.
> - II Timothy 1:3-4

Paul first mentions his state of mind while offering prayers to God - he has a clear conscience. Even though he was imprisoned and near his execution for a crime against Rome (promoting a banned religion), he felt no guilt. Like Jews in the past who served God despite persecution and false accusations (i.e. Joseph falsely accused of rape and imprisoned, Genesis 39:1-23 and Jeremiah falsely accused of being a traitor and imprisoned, Jeremiah 32:1-2). Like these servants before him, Paul suffered false accusations and imprisonment but knew that he was innocent of any wrong doing and thus his conscience was clear before God.

Paul's prayers on behalf of Timothy, therefore, are offered with a clear conscience which makes them acceptable before God. Of course the idea is that Timothy, who shares this ministry (an outlawed religion), should also have a clear conscience despite what others might be saying about the Christian faith.

The rumor was that Christians were responsible for the fire that destroyed a good part of the city. Paul reaffirms that his conscience is clear perhaps in an effort to reassure Timothy that there was no truth to this story.

Paul's prayers are motivated by the memories of his relationship and love for Timothy as a son as well as Timothy's love for Paul. Paul mentions Timothy's tears, these probably shed when they were forced to part ways after Paul's arrest and imprisonment. In his prayer, Paul asks God to enable him to see Timothy once again before his execution (II Timothy 4:9). This, he says, will fill him with joy.

> For I am mindful of the sincere faith within you, which first dwelt in your grandmother Lois and your mother Eunice, and I am sure that is in you as well.
> - II Timothy 1:5

This verse serves as a bridge to the first major section of the letter: Encouragement and Instruction for Evangelistic Service - 1:6-2:26. In his prayers and consideration of Timothy, he is reminded of the thing that brought them together in the first place: Timothy's faith and potential as an evangelist. Paul makes reference to the source of that faith and who had schooled him in the Scriptures. Both Timothy's mother, Eunice, and grandmother, Lois, are mentioned suggesting that Timothy had no male practitioners of the faith at home and it had been passed on to him by two generations of women. Paul compares Timothy's faith to that of his mother and grandmother which was high praise for these two godly women coming from an Apostle of Jesus.

Now that the subject of Timothy's faith has been introduced, Paul will go on to provide instruction and encouragement to help this young preacher's faith grow in knowledge and boldness.

15. ENCOURAGEMENT AND INSTRUCTIONS: REMAIN FAITHFUL PART 1

II Timothy 1:6-18

Paul began his letter to Timothy with a greeting and a prayer of thanksgiving where he comments on his fatherly affection for Timothy who he hopes will soon visit him in prison where he waits for the day of his execution. He then makes a bridge statement concerning Timothy's faith instilled in him by his mother and grandmother. Paul uses this device (bridge statement) to transition from commenting on the faith of Timothy's family to an exhortation about remaining faithful despite the difficulties they now face because of their common belief and work.

Remain Faithful – 1:6-18

In the section we will study, Paul will encourage Timothy to remain faithful. He has noted that Timothy, as well as his mother and grandmother were all faithful. In this passage he will list things that Timothy should remain faithful to as a way of living out the faith that is within him.

1. Remain faithful to your calling - 1:6-7

Timothy was faithful from an early age and highly regarded by the church when Paul first chose him as his helper in the work of the gospel (Acts 16:1-3). Eventually Timothy was commended (ordained) as an evangelist in his own right and continued to work alongside of Paul (laying on of hands - I Timothy 4:13-14). At some point Paul left Timothy in Ephesus (I Timothy 1:3) to continue the work there on his own. Much of I Timothy provides teaching that the young evangelist could use as he organized and ministered to this church.

The work of the gospel was challenging in itself but made more difficult in the early years because of the attacks they had to endure from the Jewish leaders who wanted to destroy the faith and those who promoted it. Now, however, it was the Roman government that was denouncing the Christian religion and about to execute one of its prominent leaders. This turn of events sent a chill through the churches in the Roman Empire and put on notice its high profile leaders (the Apostles and ministers like Timothy, Mark and Titus). Despite these threats, however, now was not the time to shrink back or keep a low profile.

> [6] For this reason I remind you to kindle afresh the gift of God which is in you through the laying on of my hands. [7] For God has not given us a spirit of timidity, but of power and love and discipline.
> - II Timothy 1:6-7

It is not that Timothy had been slacking, and Paul is trying to encourage him to preach again. Timothy's zeal for ministry was still burning strongly and Paul's encouragement here is that he should keep fanning the flames so that the discouragement of the times not diminish it. Paul reminds Timothy of the presence within him. At baptism Timothy received the indwelling of the Holy Spirit (Acts 2:38). It was the Spirit of God within him that animated and directed his ministry, and Paul reminds him of what John taught concerning the Spirit of God within man -

> You are from God, little children, and have overcome them; because greater is He who is in you than he who is in the world.
> - I John 4:4

That Spirit, Paul says, equips every Christian including Timothy with three things that enable a believer to face any kind of obstacle or attack:

A. **Power** - not just courage or bravery but the power to hold on, to endure, to suffer and even die without giving up faith or the hope of heaven. The Spirit enables us to not be afraid or broken but to remain faithful, even fruitful in times of difficulty.

B. **Love** - difficulties and suffering cannot change or destroy the attitude of love in a Christian's heart constantly renewed and enabled by the Spirit of God.

C. **Discipline** - Christians don't lose their minds or their bearing in times of trouble. The Spirit of God and His word steady the mind and heart of the believer in both good and bad times.

Paul is reminding Timothy of the spiritual resources that he has in Christ that will enable him to stay true to his calling as an evangelist.

2. Remain faithful to the Gospel - 1:8-12

Before, they could preach the gospel in the open, but now to do so would become risky.

> [8] Therefore do not be ashamed of the testimony of our Lord or of me His prisoner, but join with me in suffering for the gospel according to the power of God, [9] who has saved us and called us with a holy calling, not according to our works, but according to His own purpose and grace which was granted us in Christ Jesus from all eternity, [10] but now has been revealed by the appearing of our Savior Christ Jesus, who abolished death and brought life and immortality to light through the gospel,[11] for which I was appointed a preacher and an apostle and a teacher.[12] For this reason I also suffer these things, but I am not ashamed; for I know whom I have believed and I am convinced that He is able to guard what I have entrusted to Him until that day.
> - II Timothy 1:8-12

The choice was to preach the gospel and risk arrest and possibly death, or to be quiet and avoid trouble. Paul reviews the two main blessings of the gospel: a) salvation by grace and not works, b) the promise of eternal life.

Paul, who has preached this message openly and is now suffering the consequences for doing this, nevertheless claims that it was worth it since he has: knowledge of God, guaranteed salvation and assurance that He did the "best" thing possible. Paul doesn't want Timothy to shy away from the message of the gospel (ashamed) or the proclaiming of it either. He wants the young preacher to be ready to suffer on account of the gospel, trusting that God is aware of the possible negative circumstances that may arise in doing this, and assuring him that He is able to fulfill all of His promises despite these.

3. Remain faithful to the doctrine - 1:13-18

> [13] Retain the standard of sound words which you have heard from me, in the faith and love which are in Christ Jesus. [14] Guard, through the Holy Spirit who dwells in us, the treasure which has been entrusted to you.
> - II Timothy 1:13-14

Paul has previously written to Timothy about the problem of false teachers in his first letter, so it is natural for him to make mention of this once again but in a more general way. Paul not only taught Timothy the gospel as well as the other teachings of Jesus, he also modeled the way these were to be taught. The standard or pattern of sound words are the inspired teachings themselves. Faith and love in Christ are the way or manner these were taught, applied and lived out. Timothy was to maintain and repeat in his ministry the content as well as the manner of teaching and living that had been taught and modeled for him by Paul, his teacher and mentor.

Paul was about to be executed and Timothy was to carry on Paul's ministry of preaching, teaching and church establishment after the Apostle was gone. This would require that Timothy guard the essential message of the gospel given to him by Paul so that he could pass it on unchanged to the next generation. Again, Paul refers to the Holy Spirit as the One who will enable Timothy to maintain the purity of the message and manner it is to be proclaimed. As a normal sinful human being, Timothy could not do this, but with the Holy Spirit to guide and inspire him, Timothy would be able to keep this charge.

In the first century, before the inspired writings were completed and collected into one New Testament Canon (AD 397 - Council of Cartage), many in the church had spiritual gifts that enabled them to speak, teach and apply God's word accurately. In other words, what ministers and Bible teachers at every level do today based on their education and training in God's word, these same people in the first century carried out these things accurately through the agency and empowerment of the Holy Spirit.

> [4] Now there are varieties of gifts, but the same Spirit. [5] And there are varieties of ministries, and the same Lord. [6] There are varieties of effects, but the same God who works all things in all persons. [7] But to each one is given the manifestation of the Spirit for the common good. [8] For to one is given the word of wisdom through the Spirit, and to another the word of knowledge according to the same Spirit; [9] to another faith by the same Spirit, and to another gifts of healing by the one Spirit, [10] and to another the effecting of miracles, and to another prophecy, and to another the distinguishing of spirits, to another various kinds of tongues, and to another the interpretation of tongues. [11] But one and the same Spirit works all these things, distributing to each one individually just as He wills.
> - I Corinthians 12:4-11

To be sure, Timothy had a part to play in both keeping himself pure and following carefully the things he had been taught by Paul, but if he followed the lead and prompting of the Holy Spirit, he, like Paul, would be a faithful minister to the end. Today all those baptized into Christ receive the Holy Spirit and the Spirit does influence our lives, especially in regards to our faith. In Romans 8, Paul says that the Spirit:

- Helps us put to death the deeds of the flesh, meaning He helps us overcome sin (Romans 8:13).

- Helps us who are flesh, relate to our heavenly Father who is pure spirit (Romans 8:15).

- Helps us produce spiritual fruit (Romans 8:23).

- Helps us connect with God in prayer (Romans 8:26).
- God will raise us from the dead through the power of the Holy Spirit who dwells within us (Romans 8:11).

The Holy Spirit has always done these things for Christians whether in the first century or now. However, in addition to the spiritual help mentioned here, in the first century the Spirit also provided to certain ones in the church (teachers, preachers, saints, elders etc.) certain spiritual gifts (speaking in tongues, inspiration, spiritual knowledge and wisdom, etc.) to help them in establishing and growing churches since they did not yet have the main tool necessary to do this work: the complete New Testament.

Today, the Spirit continues to bless us in the ways listed in Romans 8:11-26, but no longer provides miraculous gifts (inspiration, tongues, spiritual wisdom and knowledge directly given by God) because for almost 18 centuries we have had access to the complete New Testament. What a few of them in the first century knew and taught from inspiration and spiritually guided wisdom, everyone can now know and teach from God's word available to all.

My point with all of this is that Paul, as an Apostle, had among his other gifts, the spiritual gift of inspiration. What he wrote was inspired by God. Even Peter, the Apostle, recognized this gift that Paul had.

> [14] Therefore, beloved, since you look for these things, be diligent to be found by Him in peace, spotless and blameless, [15] and regard the patience of our Lord as salvation; just as also our beloved brother Paul, according to the wisdom given him, wrote to you, [16] as also in all his letters, speaking in them of these things, in which are some things hard to understand, which the untaught and unstable distort, as they do also the rest of the Scriptures, to

> their own destruction.
> - II Peter 3:14-16

Timothy, on the other hand, was not inspired and we don't have any of his writings, however, what Paul says about him suggests that he may have been gifted with spiritual knowledge and/or wisdom which made him a valuable worker and teacher to assist Paul.

> [11] Prescribe and teach these things. [12] Let no one look down on your youthfulness, but rather in speech, conduct, love, faith and purity, show yourself an example of those who believe. [13] Until I come, give attention to the public reading of Scripture, to exhortation and teaching. [14] Do not neglect the spiritual gift within you, which was bestowed on you through prophetic utterance with the laying on of hands by the presbytery.
> - I Timothy 4:11-14

This may explain more clearly Paul's encouragement to guard through the Holy Spirit the store of knowledge and teachings about the gospel that Timothy possessed.

> [15] You are aware of the fact that all who are in Asia turned away from me, among whom are Phygelus and Hermogenes, [16] The Lord grant mercy to the house of Onesiphorus, for he often refreshed me and was not ashamed of my chains; [17] but when he was in Rome, he eagerly searched for me and found me - [18] the Lord grant to him to find mercy from the Lord on that day - and you know very well what services he rendered at Ephesus.
> - II Timothy 1:15-18

Paul breaks his line of thought concerning various instructions and encouragements by citing two examples:

A. Phygelus and Hermogenes - Paul likely tried to encourage various leaders from the churches in Asia Minor (Ephesus, Colossae) to come to his trial and testify on his behalf (that he wasn't an instigator or political rebel), however, none from these churches agreed to plead on his behalf, including the two men he names who probably were at the church in Ephesus where Timothy was preaching. When Paul says *"all in Asia turned away"* he is not referring to the entire population but rather all those he asked to come testify on his behalf. He didn't ask this of Timothy since he was his chief co-worker and acknowledging this at trial would put Timothy in real danger. Phygelus and Hermogenes represent those who were unwilling to take a risk for their faith. This episode exposed the weakness of their faith and is also a warning to Timothy about them.

B. Onesiphorus - Unlike the other two, this man was not ashamed of Paul's imprisonment. In other words, the Apostle's imprisonment did not weaken or destroy this brother's faith. On the contrary, it presented this faithful Christian man an opportunity for service in finding and ministering to Paul's physical and emotional needs (*"I was in prison and you visited me."* Matthew 25:36). It seems that he also was a faithful and fruitful member of the church at Ephesus. Paul pronounces a blessing on this man - that he receive mercy from the Lord in the way that he showed mercy on Paul.

And so, Paul encourages Timothy to remain faithful to his calling as an evangelist, faithful to the gospel message, and faithful to the content and manner of teaching given and modeled for him by Paul himself. He then reminds him of men, who by their actions, demonstrated clear examples of what faithful and unfaithful Christians acted like in "real time."

Lessons

1. We, as Christians, have the same responsibilities today.

We must also teach and preserve the integrity of the gospel message (saved by grace through faith expressed by repentance and baptism) as well as the teachings of Christ in the New Testament. Our task is to prepare the next generation to do this for the following generation who will continue for the next until Jesus returns. We are always one generation away from apostasy.

2. God will test our faith.

The only way we can determine if our faith is weak or strong is through testing. We never know when or how, but we can be sure that it will happen, just like the test of the men named by Paul in verses 15-16. The key to passing the test is to realize that our faith is being examined. When a crisis or challenge appears, it's not really about health or money; it's not really about justice or fairness; it's not really about success or failure. When Christians face a crisis or challenge, it's always about faith; determining if it is weak, strong, ignorant or enlightened. We pass the test of faith when we go to God for help, understanding, strength, strategy or endurance. The questions embedded in the crisis, trial or challenge are always "Do you still believe, and do you still trust me?" and the right answer is always "Here I am, Lord, use me, teach me, refine me, prepare me."

16. ENCOURAGEMENT AND INSTRUCTIONS: REMAIN FAITHFUL PART 2

II Timothy 2:1-13

So far Paul has greeted, prayed for and encouraged Timothy to remain faithful to his calling as an evangelist and the message of the gospel as well as the teachings he has received from Paul as his teacher and instructor. These were important reminders for this young evangelist who was dealing with various church issues and people at Ephesus where Paul had sent him to carry out his ministry. In the section we will study in this chapter, Paul will add another area where Timothy needed to make sure he remained faithful.

Remain faithful in service - 2:1-7

> You therefore, my son, be strong in the grace that is in Christ Jesus.
> - II Timothy 2:1

As a minister, Timothy's task was to minister or serve the church and so Paul gives him four examples of service from which he could draw encouragement and understanding. Paul refers to him affectionately as "my son" and in this we sense the ache of heart that Paul had for this young man that he had trained and mentored who was now facing the hard (and often painful) work of ministry by himself. It was the feeling a father has when he drops a son off at the airport as the young man leaves for his first military duty station. It's love and pride, fear and nostalgia for his son in the faith who is now grown - all wrapped up in one emotion. It's the catch in a mother's heart when her daughter announces her engagement. Mom is joyful but at the same time wistful and a little sad that their relationship will change forever, and the future will now bring a mixture of happiness and hurt that all new brides and future mothers experience.

As a good Christian father "figure," Paul does what Christian parents today would do: he commends Timothy to the grace of God found in Christ. In other words, he encourages Timothy to find and grow in the strength that comes from God's grace. However, what and how would one do this? Being strong in the grace means that one's strength (to do one's work, deal with obstacles and trials, endure spiritual and emotional challenges) is derived from God's grace and not personal wisdom, strength or will power. In another letter Paul summarized this idea by saying, "I can do all things through Christ who strengthens me" (Philippians 4:13).

Timothy has a difficult ministry and Paul reminds him to go to and depend on God for the physical, emotional and spiritual resources he will need to survive and succeed. Paul then provides four practical examples of those who succeed in their various areas of service:

A. Teachers

> The things which you have heard from me in the presence of many witnesses, entrust these to faithful men who will be able to teach others also.
> - II Timothy 2:2

Paul summarizes the materials, the method and the goal of his teaching all in one succinct verse. The material is the sum of instructions that he has received from Paul, from doctrine to application to Christian lifestyle. The method is to direct his efforts toward those who are faithful and worthy of being entrusted with the Word of God. Paul mentions faithful men because he wants Timothy to focus on training church leaders. This wouldn't mean that he didn't preach and teach to women in the church, but he was to concentrate on leadership training as one of his priorities. The goal of his teaching ministry was that his students would not only be able to teach others the material, but would also train others to carry on this method of teaching and training into future generations - especially those selected for leadership.

Another example of service...

B. Soldier

> [3] Suffer hardship with me, as a good soldier of Christ Jesus. [4] No soldier in active service entangles himself in the affairs of everyday life, so that he may please the one who enlisted him as a soldier.
> - II Timothy 2:3-4

The recent Secretary of Defense, General Mattis, said in an interview that the main job of the military is to win wars, everything else is secondary and every part of the military serves this one goal. Paul is saying the same thing here. As a soldier in the kingdom, Timothy's task and goal was clear: preach the gospel, plant and organize churches to repeat this cycle. As a young man there would be many distractions within the church (to major in the minors) as well as temptations outside the church (pagan immoral society and activities). If he was to succeed in avoiding both traps, Timothy would have to stay focused on who he was (a preacher) and what he was sent to do (proclaim the gospel, teach the church to obey the commands of Christ, and train leaders to train others for service and future leadership).

C. Athletes

> Also if anyone competes as an athlete, he does not win the prize unless he competes according to the rules.
> - II Timothy 2:5

Paul has already alluded to the need to the type of work and necessity of staying focused in his service as a minister. By adding the example of an athlete, the Apostle now adds the idea of "how" one does the work. Like an athlete who has to compete in a framework of rules in order to win legitimately, Timothy must teach and preach accurately what he has learned from Paul, not to mention that his life must also accurately reflect his teachings. Hypocrites may be able to correctly teach the doctrine of Christ, but they won't survive the judgment of Christ.

D. Farmers

> [6] The hard working farmer ought to be the first to receive his share of the crops. [7] Consider what I say, for the Lord will give you understanding in everything.
> - II Timothy 2:6-7

Paul's final example reminds Timothy that there is a reward attached to this service. The farmer is the first to profit from his labor and does so at every harvest. The thing he works at and with is also the thing that rewards him. He eats from what he plants and harvests. The "reward" analogy follows the same line of thinking - the teacher's reward is not his paycheck for teaching, it is the understanding he gains from what he studies. This is true for any teacher studying any subject, however, it is especially rich and rewarding for the one whose form of study is God Himself (through the study of His word) because God will bless and reward the student with understanding and knowledge of Himself; and this experience is in itself a genuine foretaste of heaven.

Paul, therefore, encourages Timothy to remain faithful in his service as an evangelist and teacher, and provides four examples of service (teachers, soldiers, athletes, farmers) in order to emphasize the various challenges and features of faithful service. He neatly bookends these passages with two references to God's role in Timothy's ministry. He has suffered false accusations and imprisonment as a common criminal. Nevertheless he has also seen the progress of the gospel and the church despite his personal setbacks.

Again, using himself as an example of a faithful servant, he declares that he is ready to continue suffering (even being killed) while remaining faithful in order to steady and strengthen the faith of those who are chosen. You become the "chosen" when you respond to the gospel with faith expressed through repentance and baptism (Matthew 28:18-20). Here, Paul adds the reward that all Christians will receive (not only faithful teachers) and that is salvation (forgiveness of sins), resurrection from the dead and eternal glory with God in heaven. Note that he says eternal glory and not eternal life, suggesting that our experience after the resurrection will not simply be "existence" or life after death but something more, and Paul hints at what that might be in the following verses.

> [11] It is a trustworthy statement: For if we died with Him, we will also live with Him; [12] If we endure, we will also reign with Him; If we deny Him, He also will deny us; [13] If we are faithless, He remains faithful, for He cannot deny Himself.
> - II Timothy 2:11-13

This is a kind of "good news/bad news" way of summarizing the different results brought forth from faithfulness and unfaithfulness.

A. The good news - verses 11-12a

If we (Christians) died with Him: He died on the cross, we died in the waters of baptism.

> Or do you not know that all of us who have been baptized into Christ Jesus have been baptized into His death?
> - Romans 6:3

We will also resurrect with Him. He resurrected from the tomb where He was laid after His crucifixion. We resurrect from the watery grave of baptism.

> [4] therefore we have been buried with Him through baptism into death, so that as Christ was raised from the dead through the glory of the Father, so we too might walk in newness of life. [5] For if we have become united with Him in the likeness of His death, certainly we shall also be in the likeness of His resurrection,
> - II Timothy 2:4-5

If we endure (remain faithful to our calling, gospel, doctrine, service, etc.) then we will reign with Him in heaven.

So here's the order of our transformation beginning at lost, unregenerated sinner condemned to hell.

1. Regeneration - born again as forgiven, spirit-filled saints at baptism.

> [3] Jesus answered and said to him, "Truly, truly, I say to you, unless one is born again he cannot see the kingdom of God." [4] Nicodemus said to Him, "How can a man be born when he is old? He cannot enter a second time into his mother's womb and be born,

> can he?" [5] Jesus answered, "Truly, truly, I say to you, unless one is born of water and the Spirit he cannot enter into the kingdom of God."
> - John 3:3-5

> Peter said to them, "Repent, and each of you be baptized in the name of Jesus Christ for the forgiveness of your sins; and you will receive the gift of the Holy Spirit."
> - Acts 2:38

2. Glorification - raised from the dead when Jesus returns and equipped with glorified bodies which will enable us to exist in the presence of God in the dimension of pure spirit.

> [42] So also is the resurrection of the dead. It is sown a perishable body, it is raised an imperishable body; [43] it is sown in dishonor, it is raised in glory; it is sown in weakness, it is raised in power; [44] It is sown a natural body, it is raised a spiritual body. If there is a natural body, there is also a spiritual body. [45] So also it is written, "The first MAN, Adam, BECAME A LIVING SOUL." The last Adam became a life-giving spirit. [46] However, the spiritual is not first, but the natural; then the spiritual. [47] The first man is from the earth, earthy; the second man is from heaven. [48] As is the earth, so also are those who are earthy; and as is the heavenly, so also are those who are heavenly. [49] Just as we have borne the image of the earthy, we will also bear the image of the heavenly.
> - II Corinthians 15:42-49

3. Exaltation - this is more than mere existence, exaltation explains why we are equipped with gloried bodies in the first place. Glorification permits Christians to participate in the Godhead.

> It is a trustworthy statement: For if we died with Him, we will also live with Him;
> - II Timothy 2:11

> 'He who overcomes, I will grant to him to sit down with Me on My throne, as I also overcame and sat down with My Father on His throne.
> - Revelation 3:21

Jesus has enabled us to share His position in the heavens. This is the final step in our transformation and reason to remain faithful - otherwise...

B. The bad news

> [12b] If we deny Him, He also will deny us; [13] If we are faithless, He remains faithful, for He cannot deny Himself.
> - II Timothy 2:12b-13

The consequences of being unfaithful are clearly and painfully laid out, and it's personal! We personally reject the faith, deny Christ, become unfaithful servants, teachers, etc. Jesus personally denies us and that denial causes the transformation to stop; our souls are then relegated to suffer without Christ frozen in the imperfect state of our sinfulness.

Paul adds a postscript here that speaks to the utter futility of denying Christ as some do quite openly and provocatively. The reality of Christ's existence and the truth of the gospel is such that a denial by man does not affect the reality and truth of His existence and position. A million people can rise up and say there is no sun in the sky, but its reality and presence is not affected by these denials, even if 20 million denied its presence it would still be shining in the sky. It is the same with Jesus. All the disbelief in the world has no effect on His presence, His cross and His promises for good or for bad.

17. ENCOURAGEMENT AND INSTRUCTIONS: REMAIN FAITHFUL PART 3

II Timothy 2:14-26

I think it would be helpful to look at our outline once again to see where we are in our study of this epistle.

Outline

A. Greetings and thanksgiving - 1:1-5

B. Encouragement and instructions for evangelistic service - 1:6-2:26

    1. Remain faithful to your calling - 1:6-7
    2. Remain faithful to the gospel - 1:8-12
    3. Remain faithful to the doctrine - 1:13-18
    4. Remain faithful in service - 2:1-7

In this chapter we will finish out this encouragement/instruction section with Paul's last exhortation: be faithful to your ministry.

5. Remain faithful to your ministry

The work of ministry was difficult especially in the first century when churches were few and far between. Christians had to deal with persecution, and in Timothy's case at Ephesus, false teachers may have been spreading heretical doctrine and plotting to undermine him in his role as evangelist and teacher. Paul couldn't be there to help in person so his letter is filled with practical instructions as to what Timothy needed to do in order to weather these attacks while maintaining unity and order at the church where he ministered.

In this section Paul describes five things that Timothy had to do in order to deal with the issues he faced. There is more to the work of ministry than these five things but Paul is not writing a general guide to ministry, he is counseling one minister about his particular situation. So for Timothy, remaining faithful to his ministry in his particular situation required the following:

A. Teach God's Word to the Troublemakers

> Remind them of these things, and solemnly charge them in the presence of God not to wrangle about words, which is useless and leads to the ruin of the hearers.
> - II Timothy 2:14

The "them" he has to remind are the Gnostic teachers who promoted a polluted gospel comprised of a mix of ideas from Greek philosophy, pagan religions, Judaism and Christianity. Their teaching content and style produced speculation and debate among those exposed to their doctrines; debates that had no conclusions since the topic of discussion had no inspired source or inspired teachers. Not only were the debates useless (in that they did not edify, provide knowledge or insight), they harmed those who participated. Constant speculation and debate over man-made ideas tends to discourage people from searching for the truth. Their disappointment in fruitless religious debate often leads them to consider the gospel message as just another false teaching similar to other lies they have heard. Endless speculation about false religious ideas breeds mistrust of all spiritual ideas, even those that are legitimately from God.

Paul wants Timothy to avert this problem by reminding (repeatedly teaching or bringing to one's attention) both the teachers and debaters of the genuine gospel message. His reference to "these things" are the concepts and teachings he has mentioned up to this point in his letter. Instead of pointless debates that neither edify nor educate, he must continually remind the church, and especially these people, of the gospel and its power to save along with its promise to exalt the faithful Christian to the right hand of God when Jesus comes. Doing this will replace useless religious speculation with the sure knowledge of God's will for mankind and the glorious future that awaits those who believe. Perhaps what is not said but implied here is that Timothy himself should not be drawn into these useless debates and focus instead on preaching and teaching the gospel which will be more beneficial for him as well as the church.

Remaining faithful to his ministry also required Timothy to...

B. Accurately Preach God's Word

> Be diligent to present yourself approved to God as a
> workman who does not need to be ashamed,
> accurately handling the word of truth.
> - II Timothy 2:15

Timothy is battling teachers and hearers who are polluting the gospel. In response to this he not only must continue to focus on the gospel but demonstrate that he is a competent teacher as well. Being diligent refers to his study and preparation as a teacher and preacher. When he preaches it should be obvious to his hearers that he is prepared, knowledgeable, and thus competent. Timothy must realize that when he preaches to the church, he is also doing this before God. He might be able to fool the church with shoddy work, but he can't fool God whose Word he is teaching.

Paul has already described the results of false teaching by incompetent teachers (the ruin or loss of faith of their hearers). If Timothy is well prepared and accurate in his teaching he will have different results:

- His hearers will be edified and grow in their faith.
- The false teachers will be silenced and shown to be incompetent.
- Timothy will not be put to shame or embarrassed because his incompetency is revealed. On the contrary, he will have confidence before God and the church that he is skilled in accurately preaching God's word and producing the results that should naturally come from this.

C. Avoid Debating Religious Nonsense

> [16] But avoid worldly and empty chatter, for it will lead to further ungodliness, [17] and their talk will spread like gangrene. Among them are Hymenaeus and Philetus, [18] men who have gone astray from the truth saying that the resurrection has already taken place, and they upset the faith of some.
> - II Timothy 2:16-18

Paul has reminded Timothy that his prime responsibility was to accurately preach and teach God's word, especially the message of the gospel. Here he adds what Timothy is not to do: waste his time listening to and debating the false teachers because in doing so he not only gave them a platform and a measure of credibility, but unintentionally caused their ideas to spread. Paul tells Timothy that his proper response is to reject and ignore them.

Paul then turns his attention to these men and pronounces a judgment on what they are doing. Their chatter (he doesn't even dignify what they are saying by calling it "teaching") is not spiritual and comes from below (the world) and not above (heaven). Their talk has already caused some to abandon the faith and return to a worldly lifestyle. Unfortunately, their ideas have advanced and this progress Paul compares to the spread of an infection (gangrene) through a body causing illness and death.

At this point Paul actually names two men who may have been at the forefront of this movement in the church. Hymenaeus is mentioned in I Timothy 1:20 as one troublemaker who was previously put out of the church, and Philetus, mentioned only here without further details. Hymenaeus was mentioned in Paul's previous letter and again here, several years later, suggesting that he had caused trouble with his teachings for quite some time. In verse 18, Paul alludes to the false teaching that had caused the problems they were having. Apparently these men were teaching that there was no bodily resurrection of the dead. Their idea was that Christians had already been resurrected (figuratively) at baptism in a spiritual resurrection to live a regenerated life here on earth with no other resurrection in the future. This concept was contrary to what Jesus and the Apostles taught on this subject.

> "for this is the will of My Father, that everyone who beholds the Son and believes in Him will have eternal life, and I Myself will raise him up on the last day."
> - John 6:40

> [50] Now I say this, brethren, that flesh and blood cannot inherit the kingdom of God; nor does the

> perishable inherit the imperishable. [51] Behold, I tell you a mystery; we will not all sleep, but we will all be changed, [52] in a moment, in the twinkling of an eye, at the last trumpet; for the trumpet will sound, and the dead will be raised imperishable, and we will be changed. [53] For this perishable must put on the imperishable, and this mortal must put on immortality.
> - I Corinthians 15:50-53

A person could choose not to believe what Jesus and Paul were saying here, but they couldn't deny what both Jesus and Paul taught: conscious, eternal life after death for believers. The false teachers argued that Paul and Jesus' teaching on this subject was allegorical and symbolic. Paul charged that they had left the truth and by doing so wrecked their faith and damaged the faith of others by promoting these ideas. For example, if there was no bodily resurrection, then Jesus didn't resurrect either. If Jesus didn't resurrect then the proof of His divinity, the effectiveness of His cross and the assurance of His promises were gone because all of these were based on His resurrection.

> who was declared the Son of God with power by the resurrection from the dead according to the Spirit of holiness, Jesus Christ our Lord,
> - Romans 1:4

People who bought into this false idea soon lost their hope (of heaven and eternal life), and their faith (in a resurrected Jesus) because these were based on a risen Savior not an allegory or symbol.

> Nevertheless, the firm foundation of God stands, having this seal, "The Lord knows those who are His", and "Everyone who names the name of the

> Lord is to abstain from wickedness."
> - II Timothy 2:19

Paul reassures Timothy (and anyone else who may have read this letter or been taught by Timothy) that the foundation (the gospel, teachings, church) of Christ stands firm despite the false teachings that were circulating.

The gospel stands -

> For I am not ashamed of the gospel, for it is the power of God for salvation to everyone who believes, to the Jew first and also to the Greek.
> - Romans 1:16

The teachings stand -

> [24] for, "ALL FLESH IS LIKE GRASS, AND ALL ITS GLORY LIKE THE FLOWER OF GRASS. THE GRASS WITHERS, AND THE FLOWER FALLS OFF, [25] BUT THE WORD OF THE LORD ENDURES FOREVER." And this is the word which was preached to you.
> - I Peter 1:24-25

The church stands -

> I also say to you that you are Peter, and upon this rock I will build My church; and the gates of Hades will not overpower it.
> - Matthew 16:18

In addition to this Paul also assures Timothy that God knows who the fakes are and who His faithful servants are as well, and this knowledge is sure (sealed). Those who are His preach and teach His Word accurately. Those who are His live faithful lives striving to be pure in this corrupted world. Without even mentioning them Paul describes the two factors that will condemn the false teachers at judgment, their heretical teaching and their wicked behavior. Paul uses this rebuke of the false teachers to remind Timothy of yet another thing he must do in order to be faithful to his ministry...

D. Flee Immoral Behavior - 2:20-23

> [20] Now in a large house there are not only gold and silver vessels, but also vessels of wood and of earthenware, and some to honor and some to dishonor. [21] therefore, if anyone cleanses himself from these things, he will be a vessel for honor, sanctified, useful to the Master, prepared for every good work.
> - II Timothy 2:20-21

Paul is probably referring to the church here (big house) and alluding to the fact that there are different types in the church. In context, he differentiates between the false teachers and their followers (earth and wooden vessels), and Timothy with those who remain faithful to the teachings of Jesus and the Apostles (gold and silver vessels). Note that it isn't God who determines the quality of the vessels, but the individuals themselves (by adhering to the proper gospel and teaching, and avoiding immoral lifestyle). It isn't expressly stated in the passage, but we read between the lines that the precious metal vessels are used and kept, while the earthen and wooden types are used for a while and eventually discarded. Based on this spiritual reality Paul encourages Timothy to be careful for his own soul's safety from the corruption in the world and distractions that often appear in the church.

> [22] Now flee from youthful lusts and pursue righteousness, faith, love and peace, with those who call on the Lord from a pure heart. [23] But refuse foolish and ignorant speculations, knowing that they produce quarrels.
> - II Timothy 2:22-23

As a man, Timothy needs to run away from various physical temptations common to all men. As a Christian, he needs to pursue and focus on right living, faith, love and peace with other Christians who, like himself, call on God in prayer with a clear conscience for these same things. As a minister, Timothy needs to avoid the kind of debates and arguments with the people Paul has previously mentioned, and instead continue preaching God's word.

This brings Paul to his final point concerning Timothy's ministry...

E. Seek and Save Those Who Have Fallen

Paul still has an eye on the false teachers and those affected by them as he instructs Timothy in how to engage these people should he need to.

> [24] The Lord's bond servant must not be quarrelsome, but be kind to all, able to teach, patient when wronged,[25] with gentleness correcting those who are in opposition, if perhaps God may grant them repentance leading to the knowledge of the truth,[26] and they may come to their senses and escape from the snare of the devil, having been held captive by him to do his will.
> - II Timothy 2:24-26

His approach should not be one where he debates and quarrels on their terms trying to deconstruct their doctrines and opinions. Instead, he is to teach God's word with kindness, patience and gentleness, correcting the errors they have embraced. His attitude provides them the motivation to listen to the Word taught. Timothy's motivation to reach out to them is the knowledge that they are trapped and condemned by their embrace of this false doctrine.

And so Paul, unable to be with Timothy in person to help deal with a destructive movement in the church, counsels this young preacher to remain faithful to his ministry, and describes five practical ways he is to do this:

1. Teach only the Word of God.
2. Take care to teach the Word accurately.
3. Avoid useless debates over "religion."
4. Flee immoral behavior and embrace righteous living.
5. Seek and save those who have fallen.

18.
WARNINGS AND ASSURANCE FOR THE FUTURE

II Timothy 3:1-17

Paul has spent the first half of his letter to Timothy both encouraging and instructing his spiritual son in the Lord and disciple in ministry. He's encouraged him to be faithful in the Lord, to seek after a righteous life, not to be discouraged in his work and to follow Paul's example of a courageous, hopeful attitude when facing hardship because of his faith and ministry. His instructions to Timothy mainly deal with his response to those in the church who were causing confusion and loss of faith because of their teaching concerning the resurrection. They were promoting the idea that there was no bodily resurrection, only a spiritual or symbolic renewal when one became a Christian at baptism. This caused discouragement and a loss of faith for many in the church. Paul's instructions, therefore, were focused on how Timothy was to respond to this teaching and those teaching it as well as those negatively affected by it. To this end Paul instructs this young preacher to:

1. Hold fast to what he has been taught.

2. Avoid useless debates and simply preach the word of God.

3. Take care to accurately preach and teach only what he has received in order to establish and maintain his credibility.

4. Have an attitude of kindness, gentleness and patience when teaching those who have been caught up in this heresy so that you will not undermine the truth of God's word with an unchristian character or approach.

Paul follows the teaching and encouragement part of his letter with a warning. The thrust of Paul's letter has been limited to Timothy's personal attitude and what has been going on at the congregation where he serves. Paul will now provide a warning concerning society, the church in general and the "times" that they live in as well as what is to come.

Warning — II Timothy 3:1-9

> But realize this, that in the last days difficult times will come.
> - II Timothy 3:1

Let's clarify what time period Paul is talking about when he uses the term "last days." In the Old Testament the Bible taught that the Messiah was coming in the future, but no one knew exactly when He would appear (Isaiah 7:14, 9:6; Micah 5:7). The prophets spoke of Jesus'/Messiah's first coming. While here, Jesus taught that after His death, resurrection and ascension, He would return a second time.

> [1] "Do not let your heart be troubled; believe in God, believe also in Me.[2] In My Father's house are many

> dwelling places; if it were not so, I would have told you; for I go to prepare a place for you.[3] If I go and prepare a place for you, I will come again and receive you to Myself, that where I am, there you may be also."
> - John 14:1-3

Jesus also emphasized the fact that the time of His return (second appearance) was not revealed to man.

> "But of that day or hour no one knows, not even the angels in heaven, nor the Son, but the Father alone."
> - Mark 13:32

The Holy Spirit, through the Apostles, provided more detail about what would take place when Jesus returned, but not the exact time.

> [13] But we do not want you to be uninformed brethren, about those who are asleep, so that you will not grieve as do the rest who have no hope.[14] For if we believe that Jesus died and rose again, even so God will bring with Him those who have fallen asleep in Jesus.[15] For this we say to you by the word of the Lord, that we who are alive and remain until the coming of the Lord, will not precede those who have fallen asleep.[16] for the Lord Himself will descend from heaven with a shout, with the voice of the arch angel and with the trumpet of God, and the dead in Christ will rise first.[17] Then we who are alive and remain will be caught up together with them in the clouds to meet the Lord in the air, and so we shall always be with the Lord.
> - I Thessalonians 4:13-17

Therefore, when Paul or the other writers mention the "last days" they are talking about the period of time that stretches between Jesus' cross (death, burial, resurrection, ascension) and Jesus' return to judge at the end of the world. Therefore, in the first verse when Paul mentions the "last day" he's not referring to that period of time that shortly precedes Jesus' return (a time that modern day *prophets* spend a lot of energy trying to predict). When Paul says "last days" he's talking about the times he was living in as well as the times we are living in today and all the time that passes until Jesus suddenly appears a second time, a time that no one knows. In other words, all the times between the cross and Jesus' return are the "last days." This is what all the writers of the New Testament understood.

> 'AND IT SHALL BE IN THE LAST DAYS,' God says, 'THAT I WILL POUR FORTH OF MY SPIRIT ON ALL MANKIND; AND YOUR SONS AND YOUR DAUGHTERS SHALL PROPHESY, AND YOUR YOUNG MEN SHALL SEE VISIONS, AND YOUR OLD MEN SHALL DREAM DREAMS;'
> - Acts 2:17

> in these last days has spoken to us in His Son, whom He appointed heir of all things, through whom also He made the world.
> - Hebrews 1:2

> Know this first of all, that in the last days mockers will come with their mocking, following after their own lusts,
> - II Peter 3:3

Paul is trying to help Timothy see beyond his own situation and get a "big picture" view of the world, the church and what the future held. Because of sin and many false ideas in the world, things were not going to get better, they would deteriorate. The coming of Jesus, His sacrifice, the teaching of the gospel and the establishment of the church along with the promise of Jesus' return was God's response to a fallen world, not a spiritually viable one. This passage may have been Paul's way of providing a "reality check" to a young preacher's inward focus because of the difficulty he was facing.

Paul has coached him in how to preserve his own faith and how to successfully carry out his ministry of preaching and teaching God's word, even in the face of opposition. In verses 1-9 of chapter 3 he opens Timothy's eyes to the true gravity of the situation that all Christians, as well as all ministers, face in this lost and dark world. In this time frame (last days) there will be difficult "seasons" or periods when wickedness will flourish.

> [2] For men will be lovers of self, lovers of money, boastful, arrogant, revilers, disobedient to parents, ungrateful, unholy,[3] unloving, irreconcilable, malicious gossips, without self-control, brutal, haters of good,[4] treacherous, reckless, conceited, lovers of pleasure rather than lovers of God,[5] holding to a form of godliness, although they have denied its power; Avoid such men as these.
> - II Timothy 3:2-5

There's a certain order to the evil and sin listed here by Paul:

1. **Lovers of self** - selfish, love self rather than God.
2. **Lovers of money** - greedy, worldly, gratify self.
3. **Boastful** - bragging about self.
4. **Arrogant** - overbearing towards others.
5. **Revilers** - angrily criticize both God and man.

These first five are the general characteristics of wickedness seen in evil people. He names more specific sins that underlie these general attitudes:

6. **Disobedient to parents** - early rebellion.
7. **Ungrateful** - a companion sin to rebellion. The first step to complete wickedness (Romans 1:21).
8. **Unholy** - no respect for what is sacred.
9. **Unloving** - without natural affection.
10. **Irreconcilable** - in the original Greek language this referred to one who would not declare a truce to end a war; couldn't appeal to this person's better nature because he didn't have one.
11. **Malicious gossips** - spread or invent evil facts or stories about others.
12. **Uncontrolled** - untamed, unrestrained by conscience or love.
13. **Haters of good** - without love for what is good in itself or good for another (envious, jealous).
14. **Treacherous** - traitorous, not loyal.
15. **Reckless** - headstrong, imprudent, rash, foolish.
16. **Conceited** - puffed up, a know-it-all.
17. **Lovers of pleasure** - the love that should go to God is lavished on self.

In verse 5, Paul notes that many people who practice such things and have these sinful attitudes cover them with a veneer of religiosity. They talk the talk and may even attend church, but aside from their show of religion they do not demonstrate the power and results of true spirituality in their lives (e.g. good works, a Christlike character, a pure life, influence for Christ in others). Paul warns Timothy to turn away (have nothing to do with) these type of people whether they are in or out of the church.

> [6] For among them are those who enter into households and captivate weak women weighed

> down with sins, led on by various impulses,[7] always learning and never able to come to the knowledge of the truth.
> - II Timothy 3:6-7

In verses 6 and 7, Paul gives an example of how some of these religious imposters prey on women with sensitive consciences who are too weak-willed to abandon their various lusts and embrace the gospel that could free them. They instead latch on to these religious manipulators who calm their consciences for a time with false religious or psychological comfort food in exchange for loyalty, money or sexual favors.

> [8] Just as Jannes and Jambres opposed Moses, so these men also oppose the truth, men of depraved mind, rejected in regard to the faith.[9] but they will not make further progress; for their folly will be obvious to all, just as Jannes's and Jambres's folly was also.
> - II Timothy 3:8-9

Paul compares the actions of the religious imposters he has just described to the two magicians in Pharaoh's court who opposed Moses' effort to appeal for the release of the Jewish people held in slavery there. These reproduced some of the miraculous signs (first three) but were unable to duplicate the rest (Exodus 7:11;22). In the same way that these two magicians (only place in the Bible they are named is here) did not prevail against Moses, the religious imposters and the general wickedness in society will not prevail against the gospel, its ministers and the church. Eventually this truth will become as obvious to all just as the failure of the Egyptian magicians' opposition eventually became obvious to all in Pharaoh's court. With this general comparison Paul ends the section or warning in this letter.

Assurance – 3:10-17

> [10] Now you followed my teaching, conduct, purpose, faith, patience, love, perseverance,[11] persecutions, and sufferings, such as happened to me at Antioch, at Iconium and at Lystra; what persecutions I endured, and out of them all the Lord rescued me.[12] Indeed, all who desire to live godly in Christ Jesus will be persecuted.[13] But evil men and impostors will proceed from bad to worse, deceiving and being deceived.[14] You, however, continue in the things you have learned and become convinced of, knowing from whom you have learned them,[15] and that from childhood you have known the sacred writings which are able to give you the wisdom that leads to salvation through faith which is in Christ Jesus.
> - II Timothy 3:10-15

In these verses Paul summarizes not only his life in ministry, but his ministry with Timothy. The take-aways for Timothy reading this passage are:

1. You've had a good example in me, keep following it.
2. Ministry is hard and sometimes dangerous, don't be surprised or discouraged.
3. Rely on the Lord in all things and He will both provide and rescue you.
4. Don't be discouraged when you see evil upon evil in the world and its influence only getting worse, this is how the world operates. Evil, degeneration, spoilage, these are the norms not the exceptions.
5. Stay focused on God's word and remember those who taught you and ultimately brought you to salvation.

Despite the evil in the world and the challenge of ministry, Paul encourages Timothy to find hope and direction in God's word which has led Timothy to salvation, into ministry and will provide what he will need in the future.

> [16] All Scripture is inspired by God and profitable for teaching, for reproof, for correction, for training in righteousness;[17] so that the man of God may be adequate, equipped for every good work.
> - II Timothy 3:16-17

Paul is always calling Timothy back to the Scriptures to provide faith, hope, courage and perseverance in trial. With these verses he reminds Timothy why he needs to rely exclusively on Scripture to safely navigate the world and effectively lead and teach the church.

1. They are inspired (God breathed). The information and direction in the Word come directly from God so Timothy can use them with confidence and authority.
2. They were given for a purpose:

    - Teaching - God's will is revealed.
    - Reproof - used to verify the truth or value of ideas and actions.
    - Correction - maintain the proper course; provide course corrections on our spiritual journey.
    - Training in righteousness - train and teach how to think and act in a righteous (acceptable to God) manner. Help the believer mature in godly character and godly service.

Despite the sorry state of the world and the challenges of ministry in the church, Paul is confident that if Timothy stays faithful to God's word in both his conduct and teaching, he will succeed in maintaining his personal salvation and will bring others to salvation as well.

19.
PAUL'S FINAL EXHORTATION, TESTIMONY AND BENEDICTION

II Timothy 4:1-22

As the title of this chapter suggests, Paul finishes his letter with various messages directed at different people and groups.

Final Exhortation to Timothy — II Timothy 4:1-5

There may not be time for another letter so Paul wants his final word of encouragement to profit Timothy for a long time to come.

> I solemnly charge you in the presence of God and of Christ Jesus, who is to judge the living and the dead, and by His appearing and His kingdom:
> - II Timothy 4:1

Paul is coming to the end of his letter so he wants to challenge Timothy to his task and does so by reminding him of three things concerning Jesus.

1. **Jesus will judge.** Jesus will be the one judging all men and women, and also judging the work of all elders, deacons and preachers. This thought should help Timothy to stand firm when criticized or attacked by those in or out of the church. Knowing that Jesus will examine your work as well as your conduct helps you when tempted to compromise your teachings in order to gain approval or promote your career.

2. **Jesus will return.** He writes, "I charge you by His appearing." William Barclay (Studylight.org) offers an interesting insight into this phrase - I charge you by His appearing. The Greek word for appearing (epiphaneia) was used in two different ways. This was the word employed when describing the manifestation of a Greek god in some way, and it was also used in connection with the Roman Emperor. For example, the Emperor's ascension to the throne was referred to in divine imagery as his "epiphaneia." Paul uses this term in yet another way that was common in that era and that was to announce the visit of the Emperor to a city or region in the Roman empire. Places anticipating the epiphaneia of the Emperor would prepare by sprucing up the town and organizing an honor guard, etc. Paul is telling Timothy to prepare for an epiphaneia, however, not one from an earthly king or leader but from Jesus Himself, the divine Son of God and Lord of all creation. Timothy should do his work in such a way that he is ready for Jesus' epipaneia (appearing) at any time.

3. **Jesus will rule.** Paul urges Timothy to action by reminding him that at some point all the kingdoms, principalities, rulers and powers will be under Jesus' rule. He is and will be the King of Kings and Lord of Lords. Timothy must work in such a way that he will rank high in the kingdom that will have dominion over all other

kingdoms when Jesus, the Lord of all, returns to judge all men and their works.

> preach the word; be ready in season and out of season; reprove, rebuke, exhort, with great patience and instruction.
> - II Timothy 4:2

In this verse Paul provides a very compact summary of Timothy's responsibilities as a preacher/evangelist/minister. His basic task is to preach God's word. The method, throughout the centuries, has included preaching from the pulpit, radio, TV, books, online, etc. and has been based on skills, training and opportunity, but the job has always been the same: preach the Word. The manner of the preaching should be urgent, whether it's to a large or small audience, an enthusiastic or indifferent audience, or a convenient time or awkward moment, the preacher should preach in such a way that the hearer understands not only the message, but also how important it is to respond since it is a matter of eternal life and death!

The objectives

To reprove – some versions use the word "convict." The preacher's task is to use God's word to point out what is wrong, sinful and worldly in a person's life so they can repent and be baptized into Christ. People don't always enjoy this type of preaching but if the preacher doesn't reprove us of sin - who will? Of course, this is not the only goal of preaching, but it is a necessary one.

To rebuke – a more modern term would be to "call out" someone for something improper. John the Baptist "rebuked" King Herod for his unlawful marriage to his brother's wife (Luke 3:19). Rebuke is like reprove but more personal and pointed. Preachers often receive their greatest criticism or lose their jobs because they've rebuked a prominent member or elder or family member of a church leader on account of bad behavior or divisive speech.

To exhort – means to encourage, comfort or rally a member or the entire congregation. God's word contains God's promises and witness of His love, mercy and generosity. The preacher needs to constantly remind the congregation of these things because we live in a world filled with darkness and death and the ruler of this world is always seeking to destroy our faith and hope of resurrection.

Paul has summarized what Timothy is to do (preach the Word), why he should take care in carrying out his ministry (Jesus will return to judge and rule), the purpose of his preaching (reprove, rebuke, exhort), the tone of his message (urgent), and finally the attitude he must maintain throughout (patiently teaching without exasperation or anger).

> [3] for the time will come when they will not endure sound doctrine; but wanting to have their ears tickled, they will accumulate for themselves teachers in accordance to their own desires, [4] and will turn away their ears from the truth and will turn aside to myths.
> - II Timothy 4:3-4

Timothy will need a patient teaching attitude because things will get worse before they get better. Paul even describes the scenario of unfaithfulness that will take place in many churches. People will grow weary of hearing sound (healthy) doctrine that teaches them to deny the world and aspire to things from above. Because they may already be influenced by and increasing their consumption of earthly things (many of which might be sinful or spiritually unwholesome) their "hearing" or conscience begins to enjoy less the teachings from the word of God. Instead of responding positively to the reproof or rebuke, instead of an "Amen" to the preacher's exhortation to move forward spiritually to greater maturity, they find someone else to teach them who will not point out their spiritual decline with his preaching.

Eventually, Paul says, their rejection of some of God's word (that deals specifically with their sins) is replaced with a total rejection of God Himself by practicing a religion not based on God's word but one based on myths (man's word).

> But you, be sober in all things, endure hardship, do the work of an evangelist, fulfill your ministry.
> - II Timothy 4:5

Paul, once again, turns his attention to Timothy and his ministry with three final exhortations:

1. **Be sober.** Means to be serious, not given to emotional reactions to everything. A sober-minded person is not led by his feelings. He has feelings but he doesn't allow them to dictate his thoughts or actions. Timothy needs to be clear-eyed, make sound judgments and not be carried away by his emotions if he is to succeed in his ministry going forward.

2. **Endure hardship.** Paul has already warned Timothy of the trouble to come, so he reminds him that when it does come he'll need to weather the storm. Sometimes in ministry you can't change a bad situation but you can always persevere. Troubles might lead Timothy to consider quitting or running away, so Paul encourages him to choose endurance over surrender when the hardship comes.

3. **Do the work of an evangelist.** Fulfill your ministry. These thoughts are connected to the previous idea of enduring hardship. Enduring doesn't mean doing nothing. Doing nothing is the same as giving up. Enduring, in Paul's estimation, means that despite the difficulties (whatever they may be) Timothy is to continue doing his job as an evangelist (proclaiming

the gospel to the lost) and fulfilling his ministry to the church (reprove, rebuke, exhort).

God will judge his work as it has been performed in both ideal and difficult situations. Paul now returns the focus to himself and, as an example to Timothy, reviews his own ministry which has for the most part been successfully carried out in the most difficult of circumstances and is now at an end with his execution at the hands of the Roman government.

Paul's Final Testimony — II Timothy 4:6-8

This letter will not only be read by Timothy but, as was the custom in the early church, copies of it would be circulated to other churches for their instruction and edification. Paul, therefore, makes his final testimony before Timothy and the church concerning his life in the present, past and future.

1. The Present

> For I am already boing poured out as a drink offering, and the time of my departure has come.
> - II Timothy 4:6

Using the language of the Jewish sacrificial system, Paul describes his death as a sacrifice to God. He refers to it as a "drink offering," the last stage of the sacrificial ritual where the priest would pour wine to the side of the altar representing the offering of a person's work to the Lord. In this sense Paul is telling Timothy that his own life and ministry will be offered to the Lord by way of his martyrdom which he believed was imminent.

2. The Past

> I have fought the good fight, I have finished the course, I have kept the faith;
> - II Timothy 4:7

Here, Paul testifies concerning the ministry he had been given by Christ Himself. The good fight or contest is the Christian life itself and the effort to live it faithfully to the end. Paul, like other faithful Christians, had successfully lived a faithful Christian life. He had completed the course set for him by God as an Apostle to the Gentiles, and done it so well that he was now about to give his life in service to his calling. He had also kept the faith in that he maintained and proclaimed the gospel as it was given to him without change until the end.

3. The Future

> In the future there is laid up for me the crown of righteousness, which the Lord, the righteous Judge, will award to me on that day; and not only to me, but also to all who have loved His appearing.
> - II Timothy 4:8

Paul reaches back to what he said to Timothy in encouraging him to stay faithful to his ministry. The idea that Jesus will judge this when He returns or appears (epiphaneia). In the same way Paul, who has been faithful in his life and ministry, will receive a crown of righteousness. This crown of righteousness is the true condition of being righteous before God, not as a hope while we inhabit this sinful flesh, but a reality once the spirit is released from the body through death. While alive on the earth I am considered perfect or righteous through faith. When in heaven, however, I will actually be perfect and righteous before God, never to deal with sin again. This crown of righteousness is its own reward, but it also signals that the eternal life promised by and through Jesus is now an experienced reality.

Paul adds that the past and present he refers to are uniquely his, but the future he describes belongs to everyone who fights the good fight, finishes faithfully and holds to God's word without change.

Paul's Blessings (Benedictions) – II Timothy 4:9-22

The instructions and exhortations have been given. The final section contains personal news, greetings and blessings.

Personal News

> [9] Make every effort to come to me soon; [10] Demas, having loved this present world, has deserted me and gone to Thessalonica; Crescens has gone to Galatia, Titus to Dalmatia. [11] Only Luke is with me. Pick up Mark and bring him with you, for he is useful to me for service. [12] But Tychicus I have sent to Ephesus. [13] When you come bring the cloak which I left at Troas with Carpus, and the books, especially the parchments. [14] Alexander the coppersmith did me much harm; the Lord will repay him according to his deeds. [15] Be on guard against him yourself, for he vigorously opposed our teaching.
> - II Timothy 4:9-15

Paul earnestly hopes to see Timothy before he is executed, and fills him in on what has taken place since they last communicated. Demas, once a faithful helper (Colossians 4:14) has abandoned Paul to return home to Thessalonica, and the way Paul describes him, has also abandoned the faith. Crescens and Titus have been sent to other works since Paul is in prison. Luke is the only remaining worker tending to Paul and serving as a link to the outside world from his cell. Mark is the "John Mark" who was on the first missionary journey with

Paul and Barnabas, and who eventually wrote one of the gospels. He has been restored to service after having left the first missionary journey early in order to return home. Tychicus is being sent to Ephesus to replace Timothy.

Paul provides a personal request for Timothy to bring his personal belongings when he comes. His cloak for the approaching winter in a cold cell; his "books" of Scripture to use at trial to argue his case concerning the Christian faith. Alexander is some artisan in Rome who was probably used as a witness for those prosecuting Paul in court. Paul calls upon God's judgment of this person because of the damage he has caused the faith by attacking Paul, an Apostle of the gospel. He warns Timothy to stay clear of this man in order to avoid getting into trouble himself when he comes.

> [16] At my first defense no one supported me, but all deserted me; may it not be counted against them. [17] But the Lord stood with me and strengthened me, so that through me the proclamation might be fully accomplished, and that all the Gentiles might hear; and I was rescued out of the lion's mouth. [18] The Lord will rescue me from every evil deed, and will bring me safely to His heavenly kingdom; to Him be the glory forever and ever. Amen.
> - II Timothy 4:16-18

Here Paul describes some of what has taken place and not just information on the coming and going of various workers. Those being prosecuted at Caesar's court could have a lawyer to help them organize their defense strategy, prepare evidence and guide them through the Roman legal system. They could also call on character witnesses or prominent citizens to testify on the prisoner's behalf or vouch for his character. Any persons that Paul could have called upon refused to come to his defense. Remember, Christians in general were being blamed for starting a fire that had destroyed a good portion of the city of Rome. Historians tell us that Nero himself set the fire so that he could redesign and rebuild the portion of the city that was burned down (Tacitus). Paul, as a prominent Christian leader, was arrested as part of the effort to punish believers for this crime.

Paul is describing how those who might have supported and defended him at trial abandoned him instead, afraid that any association with the Apostle might compromise their reputation or standing at the Imperial Court. Paul is not referring to his Christian helpers (Timothy, Luke, etc.) since these men would not be qualified to handle legal matters and had no standing at court, but rather risked arrest if they appeared with Paul at his trial.

Paul mentions a first "defense," suggesting that he was spared the death penalty at his first hearing or trial. Even though he was alone to present his case to the court, the Lord provided strength and wisdom so that Paul could make one last proclamation of the gospel to the highest officials of the Roman Empire and the crowd of prominent citizens assembled to watch the trial. Jesus' promise to provide what to say when the Apostles would be brought before governors and kings is fulfilled here (Matthew 10:19-20). Through the eyes of faith Paul sees that the message preached to these people would eventually find its way to the entire Roman Empire and beyond.

He finishes this section by noting that despite the sureness of his execution, the Lord will protect his soul so that whatever happens to his body, his eternal salvation is safe because Jesus Himself will bring him into heaven after his death. He closes out with a short doxology (burst of praise) for the Lord.

Final Greetings – 4:19-21

> [19] Greet Prisca and Aquila, and the household of Onesiphorus. [20] Erastus remained at Corinth, but Trophimus I left sick at Miletus. [21] Make every effort

> to come before winter. Eubulus greets you, also Pudens and Linus and Claudia and all the brethren.
> - II Timothy 4:9-21

Paul mentions other co-workers familiar to Timothy to whom he sends greetings:

- Prisca (Priscilla) and Aquila with whom Paul had lived and worked when he was in Corinth (Acts 18:2).

- Onesiphorus, mentioned in chapter 1:16-18 who was helpful to Paul while he was imprisoned.

- Erastus, another worker who, along with Timothy, was sent by Paul into Macedonia from their base in Ephesus.

- Trophimus, a Gentile convert from Ephesus and worker with Paul. He was with Paul in Jerusalem when Paul was first arrested by the Jews (They accused Paul of bringing Trophimus, a Gentile, into the Temple area and started a riot based on this false assumption - Acts 21:29).

Paul repeats his request that the young minister hurry his visit before winter (the end is near) and sends greetings to Timothy from brothers and sisters who are in Rome.

Final Blessing — II Timothy 4:22

> The Lord be with your spirit. Grace be with you.
> - II Timothy 4:22

Paul's blessing/prayer is all-encompassing. The Lord be with his spirit. The grace of the Lord be with him. These two include all that a Christian could ever want or need; the person and favor of the Lord ever present in one's life.

In the fall of 64 AD, the Apostle Paul was executed in Rome. He was decapitated since, as a Roman citizen, it was against the law to execute him by crucifixion. Four years later, on June 9th, 68 AD, the Emperor Nero committed suicide when he learned that he had been tried in absentia and condemned to death as a public enemy, making him the first Roman Emperor to take his own life.

Lessons

We can draw many lessons from this letter, but I leave you with two, one doctrinal and one practical:

1. Doctrinal: The Bible is inspired

> All Scripture is inspired by God and profitable for teaching, for reproof, for correction, for training in righteousness;
> - II Timothy 3:16

Most problems in church and in Christian life arise or get worse because we don't make the Bible the God inspired guide for our lives. Both preachers and saints need to maintain, defend and teach this essential truth in order to keep themselves and the church faithful to Christ.

2. Practical: Jesus will never leave you

> "...but the Lord stood with me"
> - II Timothy 4:17
>
> "...the Lord will rescue me from every evil deed"
> - II Timothy 4:18

No matter what the world says or the voice in your head says, Jesus will never leave you or abandon you. You may want to leave Him, but He will never leave you. Knowing this truth and promise is the basis for our courage and faith, and it is the foundation upon which we can build a glorious Christian life and ministry.

TITUS

Paul's letter to Titus is focused on preparing leaders to accurately teach the church and what results this should produce.

20. INTRODUCTION TO TITUS

Titus 1:1-4

The letter to Titus is the third in a group of letters (I & II Timothy and Titus) referred to as the "Pastoral Epistles." They were written in order to teach, guide and encourage two evangelists, Timothy and Titus, who were sent out by the Apostle Paul (Timothy to the church at Ephesus and Titus to the churches located on the island of Crete) to defend against false teachers, set these churches in order and appoint men to the role of elder, thus establishing church leadership.

I Timothy and Titus contain many similar ideas and phrases. For this reason it is believed that they were written on the same day somewhere between 62-64 AD when Paul had a brief time of freedom after being released from his first Roman imprisonment. The Apostle used this time to revisit many congregations he had previously established. It was during this period that he instructed Timothy to remain at the church in Ephesus (I Timothy 1:3) and Titus to remain at Crete (Titus 1:5).

The island of Crete is southeast of Greece, located on the imaginary boundary between the Aegean and Mediterranean Seas. Aside from its appearance in the letter to Titus, it is only mentioned two other times in the book of Acts:

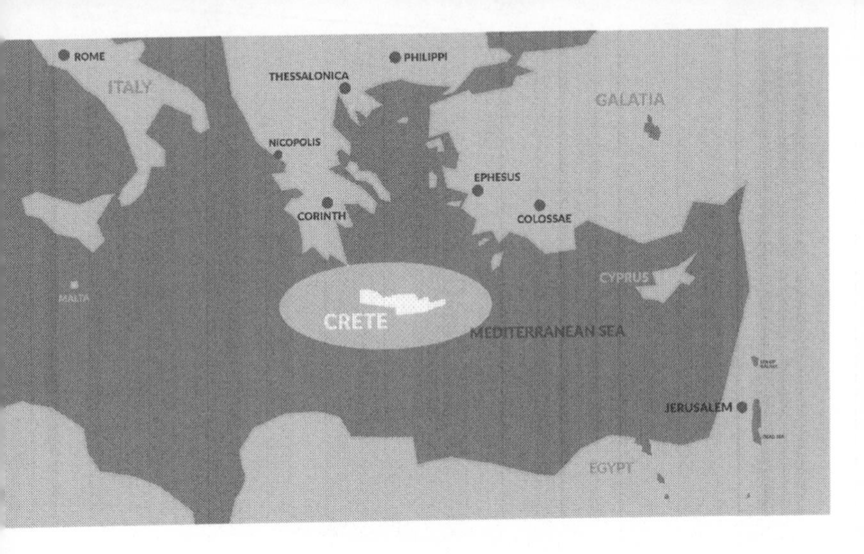

1. Acts 2:11 - People from Crete were among the crowd in Jerusalem on Pentecost Sunday. Converts made on that day might explain the presence of a church on the island some 30 years later.

2. Acts 27:7 - Luke mentions that the ship transporting Paul to Rome sailed by the island.

Titus is mentioned several times, however we don't have much background information on him personally:

A. He was a Gentile convert to Christianity and an early disciple and traveling companion of Paul.

> [1] Then after an interval of fourteen years I went up again to Jerusalem with Barnabas, taking Titus along also. [2] It was because of a revelation that I went up; and I submitted to them the gospel which I preach among the Gentiles, but I did so in private to those who were of reputation, for fear that I might be running, or had run, in vain. [3] But not even Titus, who was with me, though he was a Greek, was

> compelled to be circumcised.
> - Galatians 2:1-3

B. He was sent to Corinth to see if the problems that had existed there had been resolved according to Paul's teaching in I Corinthians:

> [13] For this reason we have been comforted. And besides our comfort, we rejoiced even much more for the joy of Titus, because his spirit has been refreshed by you all. [14] For if in anything I have boasted to him about you, I was not put to shame; but as we spoke all things to you in truth, so also our boasting before Titus proved to be the truth. [15] His affection abounds all the more toward you, as he remembers the obedience of you all, how you received him with fear and trembling. [16] I rejoice that in everything I have confidence in you.
> - II Corinthians 7:13-16

C. Paul left Titus on the island of Crete to organize the church and appoint elders.

> For this reason I left you in Crete, that you would set in order what remains and appoint elders in every city as I directed you,
> - Titus 1:5

D. Paul also referred to him a final time in II Timothy 4:10 saying that he had travelled to Dalmatia (Croatia) for unknown reasons.

We know from references in II Corinthians that Paul was fond of Titus, but his feelings about him are less noticeable in this letter to the young preacher. Unlike the fatherly tone we sometimes hear in I and II Timothy when Paul is addressing Timothy, Titus' letter is all business.

In Titus' epistle, Paul includes much of the information given to Timothy but adds sections of practical teaching concerning church life specific to Titus' ministry which is still relevant for us today.

Background on Titus

In this brief letter, Paul emphasizes one important lesson: there is a relationship between what we believe and how we act. Bad theology or philosophy produces a bad society, (e.g. Nazism = war + ruin). You can't live in a correct and productive way if you think or are taught incorrectly.

To this end, Paul will charge Titus with the task of preparing leaders who will be able to correctly teach the church, and he will provide examples of the teaching and desired results as guides to measure progress.

The Prevalent False Teaching - Gnosticism

The reason Paul takes great care in emphasizing this idea, bad teaching = bad life, was that in the first century, as in our day, there was great danger that the purity of the gospel would be polluted by false ideas thus rendering it powerless. The gospel is the power unto God for salvation (Romans 1:16) so long as it is maintained but it has no power to save if changed or perverted. This is the reason why maintaining sound doctrine is so crucial.

Today in our society we have many "isms" that war against the gospel: humanism (man is supreme), existentialism (you can create your own reality), emotionalism (follow your heart), not to mention the effects of atheism (no God) and spiritual pluralism (all gods are ok) to name a few. The pressure of these influences try to move us towards being a more worldly or ecumenic body. Maintaining the pure essence of the gospel, therefore, is a great challenge in the face of these clamoring voices often disguised as catalysts for positive change when in reality they are agents for unsound or unproven teaching.

In the first century church at the time that Titus was preaching, the pressure came from a particular group of teachers and teachings that were referred to as Gnosticism.

Gnosticism

Gnosticism is really a modern name for a system of teaching that was prevalent in the first and second century. It died out shortly after. It did not have a body of teaching, but very much like the New Age Movement of the 90's, had many strands of teachings and ideas woven into a loose system of doctrine. The strand that conflicted with Christianity and that Titus had to deal with was a combination of ideas from Jewish and Greek Gnosticism. Basically it revolved around teachings regarding the origins of the earth. Doesn't that sound familiar?

The Greeks had developed an idea which proposed that the earth was created by the descendants of the gods. In this scenario the god of darkness created the earth. They also taught that man's spirit was good and desired a return to the god of light that had created it. However, the material world, which was essentially evil, prevented this from taking place. From this basic scenario two main ideologies were developed to solve the classic conflict of the soul (man's spirit - good) versus the flesh (the material world - evil), a problem referred to by Plato as Dualism:

- **Asceticism** - A complete renunciation of the flesh in order to liberate the soul. Saturnius taught that one ought not to marry because it led to the creation of more material (children) which was bad. Paul the Apostle refers to this in Colossians 2:8-23 and I Timothy 4:1-4. Many religions (e.g. Hinduism, Buddhism, Medieval Roman Catholicism) adopted versions of this idea.

- **Antinomianism** (no law) - This taught that once the soul was released from the body through enlightenment, it was no longer morally responsible for what the flesh did. Many ancient "cults" disguised and justified their immoral sexual behavior on the basis that they were acting from a position of higher reasoning or enlightenment (i.e. Nicolaitans - Revelation 2:6-15) and thus were not subject to judgment.

To this thinking Jewish Gnostics added their particular brand of mysticism, the study of genealogy and penchant for debate which gave these Greek ideas a certain Jewish flavor. The result was a church that either:

1. Searched for salvation through a "works" oriented system driven by the Greek idea of Dualism (salvation through self-denial).

2. Was so unconcerned with sin and moral responsibility that it was in danger of losing its soul (e.g. Corinth).

Either way, the false teaching undermined the gospel and had to be dealt with by those who knew the truth and had the capacity and courage to teach it. This then, is what Paul is setting Titus up to do in Crete with his letter.

Outline of Titus

1. **Salutation - Paul's mission - 1:1-4**
    1. Preserve and pass on sound doctrine - 1:1-4

2. **Body - Titus' mission - 1:5-3:11**
    1. Appoint sound elders - 1:5-16
    2. Provide sound doctrine - 2:1-3:11

3. **Conclusion - 3:12-15**
    1. Personal greetings / instructions - 3:12-15

The letter to Titus is delivered in a compact three chapters but contains the core teaching of the Christian faith concerning the gospel.

Salutation – 1:1-4

This is no casual greeting, (for example, "hello, how are you?"), this is a statement and declaration of identity, purpose and proclamation.

> [1] Paul, a bond-servant of God and an apostle of Jesus Christ, for the faith of those chosen of God and the knowledge of the truth which is according to godliness, [2] in the hope of eternal life, which God, who cannot lie, promised long ages ago, [3] but at the proper time manifested, even His word, in the proclamation with which I was entrusted according to the commandment of God our Savior,
> - Titus 1:1-3

In these verses Paul does the following:

1. Describes his relationship to God: bond servant. Not a hired hand but one completely submitted to his master.

2. He describes his relationship to Christ as an Apostle, an envoy or special messenger. One word, "slave," describes who he is; and the other, "Apostle," describes what he, as a slave, has been given to do by God: be a messenger for Jesus Christ.

3. He also describes the message that he, as an Apostle, has been given to proclaim and the ministry that this task has produced. He begins by explaining his ministry. The faith of those chosen of God and the knowledge of the truth according to godliness are the same thing: the gospel. Christians become the "chosen of God" when they believe the gospel. The truth according to godliness (proclaimed and lived out in a godly way) is the gospel.

It is through this gospel, promised through the patriarchs and prophets, that eternal life is offered and obtained. My task, Paul explains in verse 3, now that the proper time has come (Jesus has appeared, died, resurrected, ascended to heaven as the prophets said He would) is to proclaim this good news. I do this as a slave of God according to His command, and as a servant of Christ.

For Paul this task is not merely a job or obeying an order, but a sacred trust. God Himself has entrusted him with this mission: to proclaim the gospel and teach God's word.

In these opening verses Paul has not only described his unique mission but also his credentials (sent by God, chosen by Christ). This he has done to establish his spiritual authority that he will exercise when teaching later on in this letter.

> To Titus, my true child in a common faith: Grace and peace from God the Father and Christ Jesus our Savior.
> - Titus 1:4

Paul now addresses Titus with both affection and respect. He refers to Titus as his "true child," the same expression he used with Timothy (I Timothy 1:2). He says that he and Titus have a "common faith" meaning that he knows that Titus holds the same doctrine/teaching as well as expectation (eternal life) as he, Paul, does. This point may not be necessary for Titus (he already knows this) but it is a definite signal to the church (especially the Gnostic teachers and sympathizers) that as far as doctrine is concerned, the Apostle Paul and his disciple Titus, teach the same things. This speaks to Titus' credibility before the church and other teachers.

The Apostle completes his greeting in the same way that he did in his first letter to Timothy:

- **Grace** - all the blessings of God summarized in one word.

- **Peace** - the peace that surpasses understanding that the one who is blessed experiences.

The grace is what produces the peace. The source of grace is God the Father. The connection to the grace is Jesus.

Paul writes a brief letter to a young preacher, Titus, who was working with a young congregation. They had no elders whereas the church at Ephesus, where Timothy served, already had elders (Acts 20:17). Titus faced problems with Gnostic teachers as did Timothy, but did so without the help of elders which he had to establish in more than one congregation.

Paul helps establish his credibility as a teacher and leader, and also provides him with a blueprint outlining the core principles of the Christian faith that he, as well as any of the leaders he might appoint, needed to learn, teach and pass on to the next generation.

21.
TITUS' MISSION

Titus 1:5-16

In the pastoral epistles (I & II Timothy and Titus) Paul specifically warns and equips two young preachers in how to deal with various forms of heretical teaching called Gnosticism which was circulating in many of the early churches, especially those made up of predominately Gentile converts.

A. Churches where Jewish converts were in the majority struggled with false teaching from the "circumcision party" or "Judaizers" who insisted that Gentile converts to Christianity had to first be circumcised and keep various food laws and other regulations before they could become Christians. They argued that since Jesus was the Jewish Messiah, those who wanted to be His disciples had to first adhere to Jewish laws before they could become Christians.

B. Those churches where Gentiles were in the majority also struggled with false teaching, but the heresy being promoted was rooted in Greek philosophy and referred to as Dualism. The teaching was different than what the Judaizers taught, but the goal was similar. Both groups required a "works" approach to salvation. The Judaizers demanded circumcision and obedience to the various Jewish laws as a condition to salvation. The Gnostic teachers promoted severe restriction of the body (i.e. food laws and celibacy) to free the spirit from its evil flesh and be with God.

Both of these groups were in error and promoted ideas that contradicted what Jesus and the Apostles taught concerning the gospel. The "good news" announced that salvation was freely offered by the grace of God and received on the basis of faith in Jesus Christ initially expressed through repentance and baptism (Acts 2:38). In his letter to Titus, Paul outlines the practical way that this preacher was to guard against both false teaching and the teachers who promoted these heresies:

1. Preserve and pass on the sound doctrine he had been taught.
2. Train and appoint sound leaders who would do the same.

Outline – Titus

Let's review our outline in order to fix the point that we are at in our study:

1. **Salutation - Paul's mission - 1:1-4**
    1. Preserve and pass on sound doctrine - 1:1-4
2. **Body - Titus' mission - 1:5-3:11**
    1. Appoint sound elders - 1:5-16
    2. Provide sound doctrine - 2:1-3:11
3. **Conclusion - 3:12-15**
    1. Personal greetings / instructions - 3:12-15

In the previous chapter we reviewed the salutation. In this chapter we will examine a portion of Paul's instructions concerning Titus' ministry.

Titus' Mission: Appoint Sound Elders – 1:5-9

> For this reason I left you in Crete, that you would set in order what remains and appoint elders in every city as I directed you,
> - Titus 1:5

Paul used Titus in various ways in the past. For example, he had sent Titus to Corinth in order to monitor this church's progress in light of specific instructions contained in the Apostle's first letter to them (II Corinthians 7:13-16). After Paul's release from his first Roman imprisonment he travelled to various places to preach (i.e. Crete), and returned to churches he had previously established to encourage their ongoing faithfulness as well as provide further instructions concerning their growth in Christ. In verse 5, Paul recalls the historical context and purpose for this letter to Titus. He had preached and begun a church in Crete but had not stayed there long enough to mature the groups that were formed. This task he left to Titus along with additional instructions contained in this present letter written and sent to the young evangelist during Paul's brief time of freedom between 62-64 AD.

Titus, therefore, was left to organize the church for worship and service. One of his tasks was to appoint elders in every city. We note that there is a considerable amount of information contained in just this one verse.

1. "Appoint elders" does not simply mean 'to pick or choose,' but to set into place those who qualify to lead the church. Paul's written authority gave Titus, an evangelist, the practical authority to "officially" commend certain qualified men into positions of leadership in the local assembly.

2. Note also that he was to raise up "elders" - plural. Apparently there were several cities that had churches and each church was to have multiple elders.

3. No one man was made bishop or elder over several churches or cities. Each congregation had its own leadership comprised of several elders.

Many commentaries describe Titus as the first "bishop" of Crete and argue that as a kind of "arch-bishop" he appointed other men to leadership positions who remained under his authority in the church hierarchy:

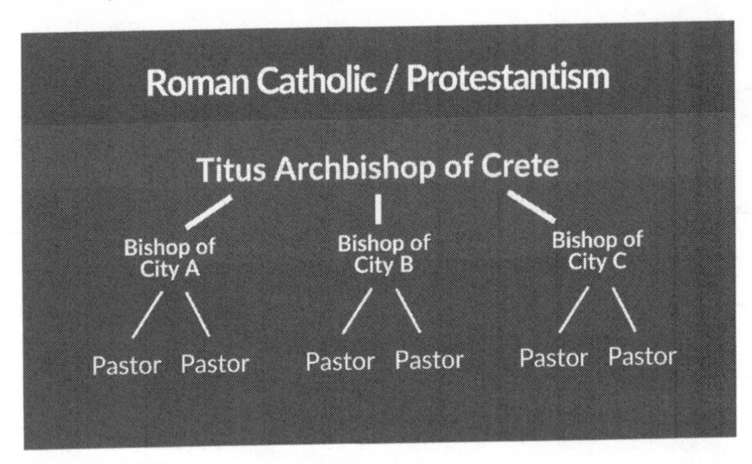

This is what you see if you look at this passage from a Catholic or Protestant denominational view; a structure that neatly fits a preconceived notion concerning church organization. However, if we view Titus' role and authority from a strictly biblical viewpoint, allowing the New Testament to speak for and interpret itself, we see a different picture:

- Titus was an evangelist, not a bishop/pastor/elder (note that Paul never addresses or refers to Titus in this way).

- The evangelist's work was to plant and organize churches by the preaching of the gospel and teaching of God's word.

- Evangelists, especially in the early church, served many different congregations who were at different stages of development.

- Titus was not in charge of all the churches in Crete, but he served all of them as an evangelist.

- He was not the arch-bishop over all the other bishops; he was an evangelist charged by Paul to establish a leadership structure in each individual church on the island.

- Once these men were put into place as elders (another term referring to church leaders), they were in charge of their local congregation, not Titus.

- We also note (by reviewing the New Testament teaching on the topic of church organization and leadership) that local elders were only responsible for the congregation where they served and no other. Their authority was not automatically transferable to another church.

Once Paul stated the overall mission (to raise up elders in every city/church) he provided Titus with details regarding the type of men he needed to look for, Titus 1:6-9. There were similarities in this letter with the list of qualifications given for elders in I Timothy 3:2-7, but Paul added more details in his letter to Titus:

1. Above reproach (verse 6)

> namely, if any man is above reproach, the husband of one wife, having children who believe, not

> accused of dissipation or rebellion
> -Titus 1:6

A man who cannot be accused of a wrongdoing or moral failure in or out of the church.

2. Husband of one wife (verse 6)

As mentioned in the study of I Timothy where this same phrase is used: a one-woman man whose married life has been clean. A man focused only on his wife having no other improper relations with other women.

3. Having children who believe and behave (verse 6)

Not only children who have been baptized but those who conduct themselves as Christians. Rebellion = disobedience; dissipation = waste. If a man has not succeeded in forming a lasting faith in his own children, why would the church give him the responsibility for the faith and spiritual life of the church?

4. Able to be a good steward over the church (verse 7)

> For the overseer must be above reproach as God's steward, not self-willed, not quick-tempered, not addicted to wine, not pugnacious, not fond of sordid gain
> - Titus 1:7

Paul has mentioned the need to be unaccused in the family or society. Here he repeats this qualification and provides details on how one acquires this reputation among those in the church. He begins with negatives, what the elders should not be:

- **Not self-willed (verse 7).** Can't take advice or correction/ has to win every time on every issue.

- **Not quick tempered (verse 7).** Able to control his emotions and his tongue; able to see someone else's point.

- **Not addicted to wine (verse 7).** Not a drunkard. Addicted is the operative word here - not addicted to drugs, alcohol, ice cream, shopping, etc.

- **Not pugnacious (verse 7).** Not a bully, easy to provoke, over sensitive, a brawler.

- **Not fond of sordid gain (verse 7).** Enjoys gambling or other forms of immoral practices to gain money. Some people will work three times harder to collect money from a scheme or a theft rather than honest work or business dealing.

Paul then switches to positive virtues that a church leader must have and must continue to cultivate:

> [8] but hospital, loving what is good, sensible, just, devout, self-controlled, [9] holding fast the faithful word which is in accordance with the teaching, so that he will be able both to exhort in sound doctrine and to refute those who contradict.
> -Titus 1:8-9

- **Hospitable (verse 8).** The word means, "lover of strangers" in the Greek. Not only offering food and shelter willingly but a person who accepts those from different cultures and backgrounds. Hospitality is one of the most effective means of evangelism.

- **Loving what is good (verse 8).** A lover of what is beneficial. Loves doing good for others and seeing good being done; enthusiastic for good work.

- **Sensible (verse 8).** Sober-minded. Not ruled by emotion. Does not create "drama" for its own sake. Prudent.

- **Just (verse 8).** Conduct that meets the approval of the Lord as our Divine Judge. A man who is just lives in a way that is pleasing to the Lord.

- **Devout (verse 8).** Devoted to the things of the Lord: His word, His church, ministry in His name.

- **Self-controlled (verse 8).** Literally means "in control of strength." This means that his love and devotion to God is not spoiled by too weak a flesh that is constantly returning to worldliness, or too strong a religious zeal that leads to self-righteousness and pride. The strength to avoid the two extremes of spiritual life.

- **Holding fast the word of God (verse 9).** The elder, like Timothy, Titus, and Paul, must maintain the gospel and subsequent teachings received from the Apostles and their disciples. They were not permitted to change, add or take away these teachings. In doing so they would be equipped to teach the church with sound doctrine and also able to correct or refute false teaching that was contrary to what they themselves taught. The elders knew, taught and defended the faith given to them by Paul and his co-workers: Timothy and Titus.

Again, not a duplicate list of what was in I Timothy but a complimentary list of qualifications that confirmed the main requirements (spiritually mature married men with faithful children).

The Need for Sound Elders – 1:10-16

Once Paul has outlined the qualifications to look for in men to serve as elders, he reminds Titus why the church needs these type of leaders.

> [10] for there are many rebellious men, empty talkers and deceivers, especially those of the circumcision, [11] who must be silenced because they are upsetting whole families, teaching things they should not teach for the sake of sordid gain.
> - Titus 1:10-11

He describes the character, motivation and damage that false teachers were causing at the church where Titus served:

1. **Character** – Rebellious: disobedient to God's word and those who teach it. Empty talkers: their teaching and opinions had no spiritual value and produced no spiritual fruit. Deceivers: they were not simply mistaken or uninformed, they knew that what they promoted was false. They were Jews (circumcision) but not part of the Judaizers/circumcision party who were in error, but believed that they were doing God's will.

2. **Motivation** – Unlike the Judaizers who were guarding their Jewish heritage in the midst of a great change, these Jews were motivated by greed and the love of money. They were religious hucksters trying to profit from the teachings they knew to be false.

3. **Damage** – Titus was told to silence (gag) them because theirs was not simply a difference of opinion on a religious topic, but teaching that compromised the faith and salvation of entire families. They first overtook families with their false notions and used this as a base to address the entire congregation. Titus and the elders he appointed should have the

knowledge to be able to refute false teaching, and the confidence to block these types from speaking to the congregation and do so without fear.

> [12] One of themselves, a prophet of their own, said "Cretans are always liars, evil beasts, lazy gluttons." [13a] This testimony is true.
> - Titus 1:12-13a

Paul quotes the Cretan (from Crete) poet Epimenides who penned these words in a hymn to the Greek god Zeus (the god of sky and thunder). It was a generally held stereotype about the Cretans which was reinforced in popular culture with this poem. (A little like generalizing about California being a liberal state or that all Canadian people knew how to play hockey.) Paul confirms this popular notion and says that the Cretans (Jewish troublemakers from Crete) prove his point and confirm the stereotype.

> [13b] For this reason reprove them severely so that they may be sound in the faith, [14] not paying attention to Jewish myths and commandments of men who turn away from the truth.
> - Titus 1:13b-14

Titus' task was to reprove them severely. In other words, Titus was to silence these false teachers spreading their lies for money, and ruining the faith and families in the process. Paul exhorts Titus to not simply appeal or bargain with these people, but silence them altogether.

In addition to this, Titus is to reprove those listening to these false ideas and jeopardizing their faith in doing so. The reproof or admonition will direct the members to stay focused on sound teaching (given to them by Paul, Titus and the elders) and avoid the useless and destructive ideas of the false teachers (myths, genealogic tables, and man-made religious ideas as opposed to revelation from God Himself).

> [15] To the pure, all things are pure; but to those who are defiled and unbelieving, nothing is pure, but both their mind and their conscience are defiled. [16] They profess to know God, but by their deeds they deny Him, being detestable and disobedient and worthless for any good deed.
> - Titus 1:15-16

Here, Paul makes another reference to these greedy charlatans. To those who are pure (purified by the blood of Christ) all things are pure. Why? Because believers know how to use all that God has created. For example, food is purified through prayer; money is a tool to care for needs and the needs of others; sex is honorable and blessed within marriage, etc. To those who are unbelieving, however, nothing is pure; they eat without thanksgiving and dishonor God who feeds them. For them, money is a goal unto itself and without its connection to God, easily becomes an object of worship or idolatry. Without the context of faith, sex is devoid of its spiritual component and reduced to producing only physical gratification instead of also being a means for creating family and a facilitator for spiritual insight as it was originally conceived to be.

Paul says that because of their disbelief and misuse of spiritual tools (teachings about God) both their intellect and conscience were defiled and thus rendered these men unable to see the truth. In a final summary statement he says the following:

- They professed to know God and know Him in a superior way. Theirs was a statement only backed up with words. A self-professed spiritual maturity and knowledge which had no basis in truth or wisdom.

- Paul echoes James where he says *"You have faith and I have works; show me your faith without the works, and I will show you my faith by my works"* James 2:18. Paul directs Titus and the church to judge these men based on their works/deeds/actions. Their deeds denied God because they didn't produce what God wanted: growing faith expressed in loving deeds (I Timothy 1:5-7, Galatians 5:6). These men were producing the opposite: loss or confusion in faith as well as a noticeable absence of good deeds motivated by love. On the contrary, what they produced were debate, division and loss of faith.

At this point, Paul ends the teaching section concerning Titus' responsibility to raise up and appoint qualified men who will lead the church, maintain sound teaching and deal effectively with those sowing division and discouragement in the assembly with their false teaching and unspiritual lifestyle.

In the next section the Apostle will provide Titus with both an example and pattern of the sound teaching he wants this young evangelist to maintain and pass on to the next generation.

22.
A PATTERN FOR SOUND TEACHING

Titus 2:1-3:11

In the first chapter of Titus' letter, Paul describes the important tasks that this young preacher must attend to so that he can set in order what had not been done while Paul was there working with him. The Apostle encouraged Titus to establish leaders (elders/bishops/pastors) in churches located in each city on the island of Crete. Titus was also instructed to silence and refute the teachings of various false teachers troubling the church where he served.

Paul shows Titus that the proper and effective response to false teaching is the presentation of sound teaching and in the following section the Apostle gives him an example or pattern of sound teaching that Titus can confidently follow.

Example of Sound Doctrine – 2:1-10

Paul begins by giving Titus an example of sound and very practical teaching that addresses the proper attitude to cultivate in order to have peace and respect among all the members in the church.

> [1] But as for you, speak the things which are fitting for sound doctrine. [2] Older men are to be temperate,

> dignified, sensible, sound in faith, in love, in perseverance.
>
> [3] Older women likewise are to be reverent in their behavior, not malicious gossips nor enslaved to much wine, teaching what is good, [4] so that they may encourage the young women to love their husbands, to love their children, [5] to be sensible, pure, workers at home, kind, being subject to their own husbands, so that the word of God will not be dishonored.
>
> [6] Likewise urge the young men to be sensible; [7] in all things show yourself to be an example of good deeds, with purity in doctrine, dignified, [8] sound in speech which is beyond reproach, so that the opponent will be put to shame, having nothing bad to say about us.
>
> [9] Urge bondslaves to be subject to their own masters in everything, to be well-pleasing, not argumentative, [10] not pilfering, but showing all good faith so that they will adorn the doctrine of God our Savior in every respect.
> - Titus 2:1-10

In this very compact section Paul addresses every demographic in the church of that era:

1. **Older men** - should be dignified and dependable in the knowledge of the Word, attitude (loving) and not easily moved (flighty).

2. **Older women** - should be respectful of God and their husbands, careful with their speech and conduct, and wise in their advice.

3. **Married women** - should be godly, devoted to husbands, home and family. They should also be

examples of purity, humility and industry at home (not lazy).

4. **Young men** - whether married or single should be sensible (serious minded - not impulsive or ruled by their emotions).

5. **Titus himself (ministers)** - should provide an example of spiritual maturity with good deeds and good teaching delivered in a humble and dignified manner. He should not give opponents (unbelievers, enemies, doubters) any opportunity to condemn his teaching or attitude. Titus' manner of living should, in actuality, cause his enemies embarrassment for having attacked him in the first place.

6. **Slaves** - slaves who were believers had a responsibility to render a good witness of their sincere faith since they were not in a position to engage their masters in a conversation with the purpose of teaching or trying to convert them. Much like a woman married to a non-believer, their witness was to be made through actions rather than words (I Peter 3:1). This would include service done in sincerity with a positive attitude. Also, they should strive to be trustworthy and reliable so that their service would confirm and highlight their faith, not detract from it.

This type of teaching did not deal with theological issues, religious mysteries or debatable topics. It was simple, even mundane, because it spoke to normal people about their conduct as Christians in every day life. However, Paul uses this type of instruction as an example of what he calls "sound" teaching. This sound or "healthy" training makes for sound or healthy members of the church.

A Pattern for Sound Doctrine – 2:11-15

Paul gives Titus an example of healthy teaching that addresses the practical needs of every church that Titus served. The Apostle then moves on from an example of sound teaching to the pattern or basic blueprint upon which all teaching needs to be based or measured against. In verses 11-15 he will summarize the essence of the gospel so that Titus can be reminded of the core ideas that will provide guidance for whatever he teaches in the future.

> *I am a supporter of 'pattern theology' (the idea that God's word provides various patterns or blueprints that we can use to do Bible things in Bible ways, or use to arrive at reliable conclusions drawn from the direct teachings, examples or inferences contained in various parts of God's word - O.T./N.T.).*

In these verses Paul provides Titus with the pattern for the basic doctrine that sound elders and preachers are to teach which will produce strong Christians and growing churches. For example, the New Testament pattern for Christian theology is contained in the teaching concerning God's grace. Here, Paul describes five features regarding grace that serve as the framework for all other teachings concerning our salvation as well as our life in Christ. Five important concepts about God's grace that need to be taught so that the church will be sound in the basic doctrine it espouses and teaches.

1. The appearance of God's grace

> For the grace of God has appeared, bringing salvation to all men,
> - Titus 2:11

The preaching of the good news, as it was prophesied by the Old Testament prophets and fully proclaimed by Christ and His Apostles. Before, men were in darkness, slaves to ignorance and tossed about by every myth and philosophy imagined. Now, however, the truth about life, sin, death, salvation, man, creation and the God who rules over it all has been revealed and been made plain for all to see.

> Now to Him who is able to establish you according to my gospel and the preaching of Jesus Christ, according to the revelation of the mystery which has been kept secret for long ages past.
> - Romans 16:25

Now we not only know who God is but we also know how He is; not a vindictive, petulant warrior or aloof creator but a loving, merciful God who is gracious and kind to sinners. Therefore, the appearance of grace removes me from the realm of ignorance once and for all. I don't have to figure everything out by sheer intellectual might, God has revealed the basic mystery of life to me through the gospel. The light that I have must be the light of grace (which reveals all of these things and more to me) or I am still in the darkness.

2. The instruction of God's Grace

> instructing us to deny ungodliness and worldly desires and to live sensibly, righteously and godly in the present age,
> - Titus 2:12

Grace not only reveals who and how God is, it also instructs me concerning who and how I need to live as a Christian. The Gnostics followed the path of total denial or the one of total indulgence in order to live in the way that would set them free from the evil of the material world. Grace, however, teaches me how to live as a spiritual being in a material world. Yes, we have to deny some things like ungodliness (disbelief, paganism, etc.) and sinful desires (disobedience to God, a focus on self-gratification, etc.), but there are many things we legitimately have access to which are pleasurable. We can, for example, indulge in things that are wholesome, good and conducive to joy and thanksgiving which are provided by God expressly for our happiness and pleasure (e.g. marriage and family). The gospel, therefore, provides me with the instruction I need to alter my ways that will enable me to live the Christian life in a fulfilling and joyful manner. My teaching, therefore, needs to reflect what grace teaches because grace teaches me what God wants me to know and do for my ultimate happiness (eternal life with God in heaven - Philippians 3:14-15).

3. The expectation of grace

> looking for the blessed hope and the appearing of the glory of our great God and Savior, Christ Jesus,
> - Titus 2:13

Paul also writes:

> We do not want you to be uninformed brethren about those who are asleep, that you may not grieve, as do the rest who have no hope.
> - I Thessalonians 4:13

The world of unbelievers has many ideas about death, many stories about seeing a white light or other experiences surrounding death and what may come after it, if anything at all. They make movies and speculate night and day about what happens after death - but they have no hope! The gospel as seen in the death, burial and resurrection of Jesus Christ brings us hope in the face of death. As a Christian, I fully expect to live after I die! There is no wavering on this point. I am a follower of Jesus because of this one hope: the promise of eternal life. Grace motivates me to look beyond this life, to make decisions based on an eternal perspective, to live joyfully in a world filled with death because I know that death is not the master over me. Jesus Christ is master over me and over my death. My hope is based on grace and nothing else; not my work, intelligence, not even my affiliation. This is what needs to be taught: that those who are under the grace of God in Christ have a true hope of heaven.

4. The purpose of God's grace

> who gave Himself for us to redeem us from every lawless deed, and to purify for Himself a people for His own possession, zealous for good deeds.
> - Titus 2:14

Question: For what reason has the mystery of the gospel been revealed to us? For what reason have we been instructed in the ways of godly living? For what reason does God allow us a glimpse into the eternal future that is grace's hope? Why has grace been established as the fundamental tenet of my religion?

Answer: That God, through grace might save us from being destroyed forever in hell. That He might restore us as a holy people with whom He would have a relationship. That He might, through us, bless others with His kindness. These are some of the reasons why we focus our teaching on God's grace which has been revealed through the life, death and resurrection of Jesus Christ, and proclaimed through the gospel.

In the beginning (Genesis) it was love that created us through Jesus Christ that we might have a blessed relationship with God and one another (Colossians 1:16). Now, it is love working through God's grace that recreates us in Jesus Christ so that we can, once again, have a blessed relationship with God and also with one another (I Peter 1:3). My teaching, motivated by God's grace, needs to reflect hope, salvation and love; not issues, personalities and worldly systems for success.

5. The authority of God's grace

> These things speak and exhort and reprove with all authority. Let no one disregard you.
> - Titus 2:15

Paul tells Titus that the teaching about grace needs to include the authority of God's grace with man. This is the pattern for the relationship between man and God. We are commissioned to preach grace and shouldn't make excuses for this. In Titus' situation, he may have been younger in years that those who opposed him with their false ideas, and this may have been used against him to undermine his credibility. The sophisticated, the philosophers, the scoffers, the legalists - all seem to find higher platforms for their messages, but they are not authorized by God. The preaching of God's grace revealed to man is the great commission and will always be needed and supported by God. If this is your message, don't be afraid! Don't apologize! My teaching needs to reflect grace without fear of men's opinion. In the end it will not be man or his opinion that judges me, but the God of grace who will judge my life and teaching as a preacher!

In the balance of the book Paul describes how the grace of God manifests itself in peoples' lives because sound teaching produces sound Christians!

The Fruit of Sound Doctrine (based on grace) – 3:1-11

A. Sound Christians are model citizens

> [1] Remind them to be subject to rulers, to authorities, to be obedient, to be ready for every good deed, [2] to malign no one, to be peaceable, gentle, showing

> every consideration for all men.
> - Titus 3:1-2

B. Sound Christians are highly motivated to live righteously

> [3] For we also once were foolish ourselves, disobedient, deceived, enslaved to various lusts and pleasures, spending our life in malice and envy, hateful, hating one another. [4] But when the kindness of God our Savior and His love for mankind appeared, [5] He saved us, not on the basis of deeds which we have done in righteousness, but according to His mercy, by the washing of regeneration and renewing by the Holy Spirit, [6] whom He poured out upon us richly through Jesus Christ our Savior, [7] so that being justified by His grace we would be made heirs according to the hope of eternal life. [8] This is a trustworthy statement; and concerning these things I want you to speak confidently, so that those who have believed God will be careful to engage in good deeds. These things are good and profitable for men.
> - Titus 3:3-8

- By their past (not to repeat it).
- By their salvation (to draw strength from it).
- By their actions (gain positive reinforcement from them).

C. Sound Christians reject unsound teaching

> [9] But avoid foolish controversies and genealogies and strife and disputes about the Law, for they are

> unprofitable and worthless. [10] Reject a factious man after a first and second warning. [11] knowing that such a man is perverted and is sinning, being self-condemned.
> - Titus 3:9-11

Sound teachers are not afraid to point out and reject those people and teachings that are contrary to grace. Many times we argue over procedure and personal issues, instead of the real issues that needs to be debated.

Personal Concerns and Final Greeting – 3:12-15

Paul finishes the letter with personal requests and instructions:

> When I send Artemas or Tychicus to you, make every effort to come to me at Nicopolis, for I have decided to winter there.
> - Titus 3:12

The Apostle is moving his workers from place to place sending either Tychicus or Artemas to replace Titus in Crete so that they can meet up in the port city of Nicopolis. Paul was probably needing Titus' help for a work there for which we have no further details.

> [13] Diligently help Zenas the lawyer and Apollos on their way so that nothing is lacking for them. [14] Our people must also learn to engage in good deeds to meet pressing needs, so that they will not be unfruitful.
> - Titus 3:13-14

We have no information on Zenas (a Greek name), a lawyer (Old Testament Law, not civil law) who had been converted and was now being sent along with Apollos (Acts 18:2, I Corinthians 16:12) who had been taught by Aquila and Priscilla. These were now Paul's assistants preparing to go on a mission of which we have no further information. Paul instructs Titus to equip them with all they might need (i.e. money, clothing, food, equipment, contacts, etc.) for both their journey and mission. These resources were gathered from church members, much like we do today when sending a campaign group or missionary out to a field of work. Paul notes that this mission furnishes an opportunity for the Christians in Crete to do a good work and produce spiritual fruit. His point is that they can take the initiative to do this and thus demonstrate their zeal in a concrete way. The exercise of giving will do them spiritual good as well as provide a profitable learning exercise.

> All who are with me greet you. Greet those who love us in the faith. Grace be with you all.
> - Titus 3:15

Paul sends greetings to Titus on behalf of all those who are with him traveling through Macedonia on their way to Nicopolis. He also sends greetings to the brethren at Crete. His blessing is brief but all encompassing. Paul uses the term "grace" here as a compact word that contains all the blessings of the Christian's faith (forgiveness, peace, joy, eternal life with God, etc.). There can be no greater blessing to bestow on anyone no matter the time or place.

Lessons

1. Sound leaders teaching sound doctrine produce sound (healthy) churches.

Churches that are dwindling, divided or discouraged are usually having problems with sound leaders or sound teaching. Sound teaching is the lifeblood of the church. Sound leadership should provide an example, a direction and motivation for the church. When either of these are lacking the result is easily seen in the assembly (poor attendance, lack of giving, low service, low enthusiasm, etc.).

2. Sound doctrine is measured by God's grace.

If your teaching content or style contradicts or does not conform to the gospel of grace, it will not produce genuine spiritual fruit. For example, "legalism" produces fruit but does so through pride, fear and guilt. Only teaching that stems from the concept of God's grace produces a desire in the believer's heart to be righteous and that desire is satisfied through faith in Christ. Grace not only creates a felt desire in the Christian to be righteous, it also enables the believer to actually become righteous by faith in Christ apart from any kind of works.

To God be the glory in Christ Jesus, the Lord and Savior of all. Amen!

BibleTalk.tv is an Internet Mission Work.

We provide textual Bible teaching material on our website and mobile apps for free. We enable churches and individuals all over the world to have access to high quality Bible materials for personal growth, group study or for teaching in their classes.

The goal of this mission work is to spread the gospel to the greatest number of people using the latest technology available. For the first time in history it is becoming possible to preach the gospel to the entire world at once. BibleTalk.tv is an effort to preach the gospel to all nations every day until Jesus returns.

The Choctaw Church of Christ in Oklahoma City is the sponsoring congregation for this work and provides the oversight for the BibleTalk ministry team. If you would like information on how you can support this ministry, please go to the link provided below.

bibletalk.tv/support

Made in the USA
Monee, IL
07 June 2023